THE JEWS: A CHRONICLE
FOR CHRISTIAN CONSCIENCE

A Chronicle for

NEW YORK

The Jews:
Christian Conscience

by HANNAH VOGT

with two chapters by Robert H. Roberts

ASSOCIATION PRESS

This book is dedicated in gratitude and sorrow to the memory of the great Jewish historian and martyr SIMON DUBNOW. It could not have been written without his ten-volume *World History of the Jewish People*. At the age of eighty-one he was dragged from his home in Riga by German Nazis and deported to a ghetto. Ill with fever, he was finally driven into the street and shot.

The Jews: A Chronicle for Christian Conscience

———

Copyright © 1967 by
National Board of Young Men's Christian Associations

———

Association Press, 291 Broadway, New York, N. Y. 10007

First published in German in 1963 by Ner Tamid Verlag, Frankfurt, Germany, with the title *Joch und Krone*. English translation by Peter Jacobsohn.

Publisher's stock number: 1625
Library of Congress catalog card number: 67-10934

PRINTED IN THE UNITED STATES OF AMERICA

Contents

5

Foreword

Christian compassion for Jewish suffering and an awakened sense of responsibility for improving interreligious understanding is no longer a novelty in our ecumenical age. But rare, still, is the Christian whose feelings are strengthened by knowledge and whose awareness of the ongoing heritage of Judaism is full. Hannah Vogt is such a person. She has written an exceptional book, and we are indebted to her for this warm, pithy, readable chronicle of the history of Jews and their relations with Christians. It should be read.

Hopefully this book will accomplish for a new generation of Christians that which Hannah's father achieved when he brought home for family reading Coudenhove-Calergi's book *Anti-Semitism*. In her preface Hannah Vogt recounts two youthful experiences that enabled her to withstand the onslaught of the Nazi propaganda. Through a reading of the Hebrew Testament she gained, early, a positive appreciation of the unique role of Jews in God's plan for history. And she was informed by her parents of the tragedy of Christian behavior toward Jews, from the period of Christian Church-Statism to the present. Such a responsible communication of knowledge is a sure defense against bigotry.

Robert H. Roberts has added two crucial chapters to the excellent account. He has illuminated the situation of the Jew in America and he has recorded those statements and resolutions that have been adopted by international church bodies as they have reconsidered Christian teachings with regard to the Jews.

A reading of history convinces one that the religious component in the making of anti-Semitism is not insignificant. But it is not just the blatant charge of Jewish culpability for deicide that is at fault. The pernicious anti-Judaic stereotype of the Pharisees as "legalists" and "hypocrites," the conviction that Judaism is a corrupt religion, an insufficient vehicle for God's witness to the world, and that the church has replaced a rejected synagogue in God's salvation history —such attitudes, coupled with no awareness of how Judaism has progressed, changed, and deepened since the Jewish-Christian schism, are truly the seed bed of the ugly weed that is Jew-hatred.

The churches have at last correctly interpreted the crucifixion account so that Jews will no longer have to shoulder the burden of a sinfulness within the capacity of every man. But Christians are only beginning to glimpse behind the ghetto wall to discover the spiritual richness of God's ongoing conversation with the Jewish people. A more secure Jewish-Christian relationship will be built only upon the foundation of such knowledge.

A reading of history informs us also how frequently men have misused religion in order to sanctify their distorted political and economic ambitions. A study of Hannah Vogt's book will make such misuse much less a possibility.

Much of anti-Semitism has nothing to do with religion. Yet Jews remain a target in western civilization. Is it not because they are a people unique in God's self-revelation to mankind? Anti-Semitism is a denial of God; it is a repudiation of true religion. Ultimately, therefore, the problem of anti-Semitism and race prejudice, poverty, and war will be overcome when men hear what God speaks to the conscience through his dealings with Jews and through Jews with the nations of the world; and certainly we must consider its dealings with the church that calls itself "New Israel" and its relationship to the world. Hannah Vogt's book is intended to help us listen.

RABBI ARTHUR GILBERT

Introduction

> Love is patient; love is kind and envies no one. Love is
> never boastful, nor conceited, nor rude; never selfish, not
> quick to take offence. Love keeps no score of wrongs; does
> not gloat over other men's sins, but delights in the truth.
> There is nothing love cannot face; there is no limit to its
> faith, its hope, and its endurance (I CORINTHIANS 13:4–7).

"These findings allow only one conclusion: Not only do the vast
majority of Christian church members exhibit an affinity for anti-
Semitic beliefs, but nearly half frankly admit to anti-Semitic
feelings," write Charles Y. Glock and Rodney Stark in their com-
prehensive study *Christian Beliefs and Anti-Semitism.*

Christians must face up to the problem of anti-Semitism. It is
possible to learn a great deal about the nature and causes of anti-
Semitism from a psychological, economic, or sociological perspec-
tive. Yet for anyone interested in religion in general, or in
Christianity in particular, a fundamental question remains: How
can it be that a religion, grounded in love for God and neighbor
could be guilty of the inhuman persecution of the Jews over a
period of twenty centuries? To point out that the Jews were persecuted before the advent of Christianity, or under Islam, is to
evade the issue. The tragic story of the church's failure cannot be

atoned by references to historical occasions when Christians have acted in love toward their Jewish neighbors. Nor is it satisfactory to claim that Christians who are anti-Semitic are not "authentic." This claim simply raises the question of why the Christian religion has produced such an abundance of inauthentic Christians. Nothing can alter the historical fact that anti-Semitism flourishes in the Christian atmosphere. It is both persistent and omnipresent in the Christian world.

Why must the Christian church be concerned with its relationship to the Jews? Because anti-Semitism is a sin against God and man and a violation of the Christian command for love of neighbor. Christianity and anti-Semitism are theoretically antithetical. Both Jews and Christians are fellow creatures of God, and there can be no possible theological foundation for hatred between them. In the words of the New Testament, "But, if a man says, 'I love God,' while hating his brother, he is a liar" (I John 4:20). Surely any mature interpretation of the Christian faith would emphasize the universality of the word *brother.*

Then too it is clear historically that Christianity is inseparably bound up with the people of Israel. Christianity is an offspring of Judaism. Indeed, it is impossible to understand Christianity without a knowledge of Judaism. Jesus of Nazareth, to the Christians the promised Messiah, was himself a Jew. Educated according to the customs of the Jewish home and synagogue, Jesus was a product of first-century Judaism. Mary and Joseph had their first-born circumcised according to the Law. Jesus observed Passover, made pilgrimages to the Temple in Jerusalem, attended the synagogue, and was viewed by his contemporaries as a rabbi. Indeed, Jesus' ethical precepts were basically the ethics of the Jewish oral tradition as it had existed in some form since the time of Ezra.

The earliest Christians were all Jews who maintained the Jewish holy days, read and studied the Torah, and practiced such Jewish religious laws as circumcision, the observance of the Sabbath, and the eating of kosher foods. If all the quotations from and references to the Jewish Bible were taken out of the Christian Bible there would be little remaining, for the New Testament writers validated their religious claims on the authority of their interpretation of the

Scriptures of Israel. Christianity has adopted the heroes of the Jewish Bible for its own. Many Christians tend to think of Abraham, Moses, David, and Jeremiah as sort of pre-Christ Christians. But they were not. They were Jews, who found their religious resources within Judaism. Authentic Christianity glories in its Jewishness—rooted as it is in the revelation of God to the children of Abraham, Isaac, and Jacob.

There is another reason to think of anti-Semitism as a Christian problem—the church is and has been an accessory to the crime of hatred against the Jews. It has for two thousand years dealt with the Jews in an unchristian fashion.

The sordid story of Christian hatred for the kin of Jesus ranges from subtle acts of discrimination to mass murder. Some of the most illustrious names of church history have fostered this hatred from patristic times. The ghetto and the yellow star were implements of the Christian persecution of the Jews long before the Nazi reign of terror. Christianity has played a sinful role in the development of that diabolical force which in our time sent six million Jews to the furnaces of Auschwitz and Treblinka. The "final solution" to the "Jewish problem" was arrived at in a classical Christian country, a country steeped in Christian tradition. On Sunday mornings in those horror-filled days of the late 1930's and early 1940's many of the seven thousand persons employed at Auschwitz took their wives and children to Protestant or Catholic Churches and prayed, ". . . thy will be done on earth as it is in heaven."

And lest we begin to feel little personal responsibility for this unbelievable slaughter it behooves us to remember the failure of Christians of the world, as well as the governments of Britain and the United States, to face realistically the fact of Jewish destruction and to rise to the opportunity to help those who escaped.

Anti-Semitism is still very much alive today. The tragic results of this form of group hatred witnessed by our generation have not cured us of the disease. And the Christian church continues to provide the culture in which this germ may grow. In 1966 Charles Y. Glock and Rodney Stark, two social scientists who had conducted intensive research into the relationship of Christianity and anti-Semitism in America, expressed their personal feelings in this way: "But as the findings were revealed, both of us shared equally a sense of shock and dismay that a faith which proclaims the brotherhood of man can be so perverted into a *raison d'etre* for bigotry." This study declares that Christian teachings continue to enforce and foster anti-Semitic attitudes in the United States.

Unfortunately many contemporary Christians are unaware of this aspect of the church's history. These pages have been omitted from our history books. Most Christians know of the suffering Christian martyrs endured for their faith and they are aware of historical and contemporary persecutions of Christians, but of the persecution of the Jews perpetrated by Christians, most Christians are ignorant.

This blind spot is tragic for two reasons. First it reveals a lack of knowledge of what has happened to the Jews. The history of the Jewish people did not come to an end with the birth of the church. Judaism is not a fossilized religion. Christians must become increasingly aware of the two thousand years of postbiblical Jewish history. We must discover what God is saying to the nations through this people.

Second, our ignorance of Christianity's anti-Semitic guilt prevents us from seeing ourselves as we really are. We too readily edit out of our history actions for which we need feel shame. And by so doing we build up a distorted image of our past. Only when we know the historical facts can we begin to ask some pertinent questions. Why does the Christian need the image of the Jew that he has created? Is there an inherent weakness in Christianity that requires anti-Semitism? Why does the Christian feel the need to persecute the Jew? Is it possible for the Christian to treat the Jew simply as a human being rather than as the classic villain of Christian lore?

Confrontation with the historical record will help Christians acknowledge that anti-Semitism is a Christian problem. Thus Hannah Vogt's book, *The Jews: A Chronicle for Christian Conscience,* is very important. This work is an important contribution to the Christian's understanding of the Jew and of himself, for the story of the Jews in western civilization is one of Christian oppression. Miss Vogt has covered the most outstanding events magnificently in just a few pages. An attitude of authentic Christian concern is reflected throughout the telling of this sad tale.

The story as told here is not, however, complete. There is

another dimension to Jewish history besides the heroic response and suffering in the face of Christian oppression. The Jew has been more than a victim—he has been a generous contributor to the thought and development of western civilization. Jewish men and women have made immense contributions in all fields of human endeavor: medicine, mathematics, chemistry, physics, philosophy, the arts, philanthropy, education, finance, business, politics, and government are just a few examples.

The Jews: A Chronicle for Christian Conscience is a partial history limited to only one aspect of the story of the Jewish people. Its purpose is to help Christians understand something of the story of the Jews and most particularly to tell them of the wrongs perpetrated against the Jews in our Christian-influenced society.

Such a story is told as an act of love and it must be received in a spirit of penitence and reconciliation so that Christians might undertake the revision of teaching and attitudes, to inaugurate a new pattern of authentic Christian relationship towards their Jewish neighbors. Good Christian theology teaches that repentance precedes redemption. It is to be hoped that the retelling of the tragic story of the Jews will bring us as Christians to genuine repentance that will motivate us to redeem our attitudes and actions towards our Jewish brothers.

THE REVEREND ROBERT H. ROBERTS

PREFACE TO THE AMERICAN EDITION

"Why have you, a Christian, written this book?" the American publishing house inquired. For an answer, I have to go back to my youth, for I am sure that my love for Jewry has its roots there. I had just learned to read when I was given a children's Bible, illustrated with drawings by Schnorr von Carolsfeld. I have read it again and again, and the stories of the patriarchs, the wonderful legend of Joseph, the deliverance of the people by Moses, David's friendship with Jonathan, the great wisdom of Solomon and the splendor of his Temple—all these became my ever-present and vivid possession. Although I shed bitter tears on the crucifixion of Jesus, I never had the idea that "the Jews" were guilty of this. I regret losing this little volume, for it certainly was a pedagogically superb work.

When I was about fifteen or sixteen years old, my father brought from the Göttingen University Library, where he worked, a book by Richard Coudenhove-Calergi, the great European, which bore the title *Anti-Semitism*. It was from this book that I first learned of the fate of the Jews during the Crusades. I read about the Jewish communities of Worms and Mainz, which sacrificed themselves in honor of the Holy Name together with their aged, their women, and their children. Their martyrdom touched me even more since it had never been thought necessary to tell us of it in our history lessons. It became plain to me how deeply Christian prejudice had influenced the values in this regard, where the same loyalty and steadfastness that we had learned to admire with holy shudder when we read of the Christians being burned in Nero's gardens was, when found to be characteristic of the Jews in similar crises, dismissed as "impenitence," robbed of all its glamor, and not even found worthy of mention. I understood why the small minority of Jews did not perish, and again and again triumphed over the brutality and superstitious obsession of their persecutors. "To persevere and to remain, as the community which makes no concessions, to exist in the world and yet be different from them, to be present as the receptacle of power, this was the task which for all these centuries has been fulfilled by an incomparable seriousness of presence, an unshakable vital energy." This is how, very much later, Leo Baeck in his book *Das Wesen des Judentums* ("The Es-

15

sense of Judaism") interpreted to me the existence of the Jewish people, which borders on a miracle.

Later, there came the economic crisis, and anti-Semitism in Germany became ever louder and more brazen. What I thought about it is shown by a letter of May, 1930, of which I retained a copy by mere chance:

There will be a National-Socialist (Nazi) meeting on Sunday. I shall probably go there, but will certainly itch all over. One actually itches, in the fists and in the throat, when one has to listen to these people, without being able to defend oneself against them that very minute. Just the fact that Jews, who are being used by all Nazis as the patient whipping boys (scapegoats), who are guilty of capitalism as well as of communism, of banking and usury, of bad literature, and simply of everything that was a failure, that these very Jews are being denied any possibility of reply, that the simple *et altera pars* ["and the other party"] is so maliciously denied, this alone will always prevent me from becoming a National Socialist (Nazi). I would be ashamed to make such cheap agitation.

Three years later, National Socialism came to power. My Jewish and "half-Jewish" friends left the country. They recognized in time the danger threatening them. I learned of the full extent of the incomprehensible crimes against Jewry only after 1945. I never had any illusions about Theresienstadt (Terezin), but that there also was an Auschwitz, I still had to learn.

Since then, one question has given me no rest: Would Hitler have succeeded in finding so many yes-sayers and so many accomplices, if more people had known and lived the history of Jews as I have? And I am filled with one hope: Will there be in the future some young Germans, not saddled with guilt, who will grasp the great loss and the grief at what Hitler robbed from the German people by destroying the more-than-one-thousand-year-old coexistence of Jews and Germans?

From this question and this hope was created this little book, which was written for the young generation in Germany, but which will—I hope—also be given a friendly reception in the country that has offered protection and a home to so many Jews expelled from Europe.

HANNAH VOGT

Göttingen

1

The People of the Old Covenant

The Exodus From Egypt

The events which the Jews relive every year at Passover are essentially based on historical facts, even though they are tinged with legend. Not only the Bible but also Egyptian documents record that nomadic tribes from the neighboring deserts often crossed into Egypt with their herds of sheep and goats in time of drought; it was their only hope of escaping famine. Egypt, thanks to the Nile floods, was the granary of the East. It can therefore be assumed that the royal border officials also admitted the tribes whom the Egyptians called *Habiru,* or "Hebrews," and who called themselves "Israel" (after one of their tribal ancestors), which means: "He who strives with God." Permission was usually not granted without a tribute being exacted, either livestock or labor. Labor was always in great demand in Egypt. The monumental tombs of the Pharaohs, the pyramids, and the large temple cities for the many gods in animal form required tens of thousands of slaves. One of the most prodigious among the royal builders was Ramses II (ca. 1300–1225 B.C.). He started construction of huge temples and of whole cities for grain storage, particularly in the province which is mentioned as the Land of Goshen in the Bible. It is generally assumed that he was the Pharaoh who forced the Israelite tribes, which had immigrated about two generations earlier, to work in his brickyards. Regular servitude under the whip of an Egyptian overseer was intolerable for the proud and free

17

sons of the desert. Obviously, they wanted nothing as much as escape from bondage.

In their adversity they found a leader among their own people. His name, Moses, is of Egyptian origin and indicates that he was raised at the Royal Egyptian court. Having killed one of the slave masters in anger, he had to flee into the desert, where he was welcomed by another tribe, the Midianites. Here in the solitude of the desert he had an exalted vision. From a burning bush he heard the voice of God, whom the fathers of his people had revered under various names and who now made himself known to him as YHWH—an arcane word which can mean "The One Who Is"—and who commanded him to lead the Israelites out of Egypt. Though Moses did not feel equal to the task, he obeyed the call and returned to his persecuted people. We have no historical record of whether and how often Moses negotiated with the Pharaoh for the deliverance of his people and what events finally favored their escape. Here the core of historical truth has been much embroidered by the imagination of the faithful. It is certain, however, that the flight had to be carried out in the greatest haste. The Sea of Reeds near the Bitter Lakes, which were then still connected with the Red Sea, had been dried out by a favorable wind so that the Israelites reached the opposite shore, while the pursuing Egyptian army was caught by the returning waters, and perished.

It is idle to debate whether this deliverance can be explained by natural causes or not. But it is decisive for the entire subsequent history of the Hebrew tribes that they regarded their deliverance as the act of the God whom Moses had made known to them.

> "I will sing to the LORD, for he has triumphed gloriously;
> The horse and his rider he has thrown into the sea."
> —Exodus 15:1b

This brief song of praise, which originated then and which the rescued Israelites sang in unending repetitions to the sound of drums and cymbals, is the expression of their gratitude and awe. *They glorified, not Moses, the leader and seer, but the God for whom Moses was only mouthpiece and tool.*

The Laws and the Covenant

From the Sea of Reeds Moses led the people to Kadesh, one of the largest oases on the Sinai peninsula. Here the Israelitic tribes remained for many years. (The Bible says forty, but in Hebrew forty is also an indefinite number, like our word *many*. Probably they remained there and in the surrounding desert until a new generation had grown up.) During these years Moses completed his work. He announced God's will to his people, and he laid down the directions according to which they were to live in the future.

He reinstituted the custom of circumcision as a sign of the covenant between God and this people. It was a custom that went back to the patriarch Abraham, and was also practiced by other tribes. He issued rules for the conduct of marriages, for the arbitration of disputes, for the treatment of servants and especially of strangers: "You shall not wrong a stranger or oppress him, for you were strangers in the land of Egypt" (Exodus 22:21). But he also laid down rules regarding everyday matters, such as eating, drinking, and cleanliness. Not every animal was to be eaten; some animals, among them pigs, were classed as unclean and forbidden as food. Pagan customs, such as cooking a freshly killed lamb in its mother's milk, were forbidden. Later this prohibition was taken to mean that milk and meat could never be eaten together and that even the dishes and cutlery for milk and meat had to be kept strictly separate. The blood of animals could not be eaten, and this required a special kind of slaughter: windpipe and gullet of the animal had to be severed swiftly; the animal became unconscious instantly and the blood drained out completely. Other rules concerned cleanliness, which every individual had to observe, both for himself and for the camp. Included were the ritual ablutions that served as purification after contact with unclean objects.

But above all these rules tower in awesome grandeur and brevity the Ten Commandments, which Moses is said to have brought down on stone tablets from the fire-and-smoke-encircled heights of Mount Sinai:

> I the Lord am your God who brought you out of
> the land of Egypt, the house of bondage.

You shall have no other gods beside Me.

You shall not swear falsely by the name of the
Lord your God.

Remember the sabbath day and keep it holy.

Honor your father and your mother.

You shall not murder.

You shall not commit adultery.

You shall not steal.

You shall not bear false witness against your
neighbor.

You shall not covet your neighbor's house:
you shall not covet your neighbor's wife, or his
male or female slave, or his ox or his ass, or
anything that is your neighbor's.

—Exodus 20:2–17

At Mount Sinai Moses revealed to the people that God wanted
to enter into a covenant with them:

"Now therefore, if you will obey my voice and keep my
covenant, you shall be my own possession among all peoples;
for all the earth is mine, and you shall be to me a kingdom
of priests and a holy nation."

—Exodus 19:5–6a

By this act the Jews became the "Chosen People." The term has
often been maliciously misinterpreted, yet it has nothing to do
with the virtues or merits of this people, its strength or its glory.
To be chosen entailed obligations and required adherence to the
commandments, renunciation, and obedience.

From the biblical chroniclers we learn that neither vanity nor
self-flattery played a role here. They tell us that from the very first
day the Chosen People failed again and again to live up to the
demands of their God. In the Land of Goshen the Israelites had
come to know the cat-, dog-, and ibis-headed idols of the Egyptians,
and their worship before these graven images. When Moses brought
down the tablets of the Law from Mount Sinai, it is told, the people

were dancing around the graven image of a golden calf and shouting, "These are the gods that have led us out of Egypt!"

God had shown himself to Moses as all-present and all-powerful. As a sign of his presence, the Ark of the Covenant was fashioned. This Ark, marked by the figures of two cherubs, became the repository of the tablets of the Law. The Ark was kept in a special tent, and always accompanied the Israelites when they moved on or waged war.

Moses has often been compared to a stone mason. Under his powerful hammer blows, hordes of fugitive slaves were fashioned into a people gathered around a summoning, demanding, invisible God. Often the Bible speaks of grumbling and discontent, of insubordination and revolt, and of despondency among the children of Israel. With justice and wisdom, with wrath and patience, the great national leader and man of God succeeded in holding the growing nation together. Finally he showed them the way, though he was not destined to accompany them. He bade them conquer the Land of Canaan, the land promised to their forefather Abraham.

Settlement in the Land of Canaan

History has known many similar conquests: Warlike nomadic tribes invade the fertile lands of agricultural peoples, subjugate them, intermingle with them, and themselves become settled. After the Israelitic tribes had largely reached their goal, the warrior leader of the northern tribes, Joshua, summoned the leaders of the twelve tribes to an assembly at Shechem. There he asked them whether they were willing to fear God and serve him. If not, they were free to chose other gods for themselves. All the tribes vowed that they would serve the one God, even though Joshua told them that it was not easy to serve *YHWH,* who was a jealous God, a God who demanded loyalty to himself alone and punished half-measures and defections. Following this renewal of the Covenant, Joshua laid down laws and statutes for all the tribes.

Politically, the tribes remained a loose federation. They came to each other's aid when their territory had to be defended against invading tribes. Particularly brave and successful leaders like Deborah, the judge, and Gideon, the farmer's son, were regarded as leaders sent by *YHWH*. The Israelites had received their laws directly from God, and hence no ruler was to stand between them and God. When they asked Gideon to become King, he answered, "I will not rule over you . . . the LORD will rule over you" (Judges 8:23). This consciousness of being ruled directly by God characterized the federation of the twelve tribes.

Yet this loose federation, lacking strong leadership, could not hold its own when the Philistines invaded the country. As part of a mass transmigration, they had come from the Aegean isles and settled on the coast of Canaan. Egyptian reliefs show the Philistines as tall and warlike. Their superiority over the Israelites was based primarily on their ability to forge tools of iron. In their first great encounter they defeated the Israelite army, carried off the Ark of the Covenant, and destroyed the Shrine of Shilo. After this national catastrophe the tribes clamored for a central and permanent leadership: ". . . now appoint for us a king to govern us like all the nations" (I Samuel 8:5b).

The Kingdom

For sixty years the Philistines were the undisputed rulers of the country, which has since been named after them: Philistine-Palestine. Then Saul, a warrior from the tribe of Benjamin, waged a victorious campaign against the Ammonites east of the Jordan—probably with the consent of the Philistines. After the victory Saul did not dismiss his men. Instead, as soon as an opportunity presented itself, these experienced fighters turned against the Philistines. Saul was the first to be anointed King of Israel. He was a powerful warrior and a highly gifted strategist. During the entire twenty years of his reign, the last of which were darkened by mental depressions, he had to fight the Philistines; eventually he and three sons died in battle at Mount Gilboa.

His only surviving son, who was still under age, did not succeed him. The new king was a man whom Saul had called to his court to divert him by playing the harp, and whom he later persecuted as single-mindedly as he had formerly given him his trust. This man was David, the husband of Saul's daughter Michal and the friend of Saul's son Jonathan. David had to hide from the King's wrath with a band of companions in arms from his own tribe of Judah, leading for many years the precarious existence of a partisan chieftain.

He may have been regarded by some of the tribes as pretender to the throne, even during Saul's lifetime, which might also explain Saul's enmity. In any event, David was immediately made King in Judah, though the northern tribes acknowledged him as their king only later. While David had to continue to wage war, he could build on Saul's political accomplishments and devote more of his time to strengthening the Kingdom of Israel internally. A most important achievement was the conquest of Jerusalem and the establishment of a new central sanctuary there. The Ark of the Covenant had in the meantime been recaptured from the Philistines. With the King himself dancing and singing before it, it was carried ceremoniously into the new sanctuary and installed in a tent in commemoration of the original tabernacle. Jerusalem soon outshone all other tribal shrines and became the political and religious center of Israel.

To his people David became the prototype of the ideal king. Yet the chroniclers have not hesitated to portray his defects. His offense against Uriah and Bathsheba, his weakness toward his sons, the hatred he bore his faithful commander-in-chief, Joab, even beyond the latter's death, and many other failings cast an ambiguous light on his character. Yet the chroniclers also described his great gift in dealing with people, his intelligence, the charm of his poetic and dazzling personality. Above all, however, David was a "ruler under God." He acknowledged himself to be a sinner and bowed humbly before *YHWH,* the only "King of Glory." It is no coincidence that when the people later yearned for a savior with divine authority, their desire was linked with the name of David.

His son and successor, Solomon, also became a favorite subject of legend, but in an entirely different sense. He was admired for his extraordinary intelligence, which enabled him to settle the most difficult legal problems and to solve every riddle. Countless sayings of wisdom and rules of conduct are attributed to him. But at the same time he is portrayed as a ruler with an oriental love of display, including a large harem. The costs had to be met by rising taxes, which were collected by a skilled administration. Solomon also built the Temple, one of the architectural wonders of the ancient world, and into its holy of holies he placed the Ark of the Covenant. Yet essentially Solomon's reign was far more worldly than David's, much further removed from God. When he died after a reign of forty years, it became evident that the externally magnificent edifice of the kingdom had begun to rot. In the very same year (922 B.C.) it broke asunder: into the northern kingdom, which consisted of ten tribes and called itself Israel, and the southern kingdom, which comprised Jerusalem and was based mainly on the ancient tribal lands of Judea.

The larger northern kingdom was initially ruled by a former overseer of slaves, Jeroboam, and then by a number of elected kings, many of whom died violently. The northern kingdom became quickly entangled in power politics. By means of changing alliances it tried to maneuver between the great powers. Each of these powers had its partisans in Israel, and palace intrigues, revolts, and political murders were the result. Foreign influence found its most visible expression in the worship of foreign gods.

Some two hundred years after Solomon's death the northern kingdom fell victim to a punitive expedition of the Assyrians. The King was taken prisoner, and a large part of the population was deported into distant regions of the Assyrian Empire. There they vanished without trace, which later led to many fantastic conjectures. Again and again people believed that in a hitherto unknown tribe in China, India, or America they had rediscovered the ten lost tribes. The truth is probably simpler: the deported ten tribes likely merged with the nations among whom they lived. Although there had been prophets in the northern kingdom who had tried to recall the people to God, the religious intermingling had assumed such proportions that among strangers the faith in the one, invisible God failed to conserve and keep the Israelites as a people apart.

The Prophets

The appearance of the prophets in the northern and southern kingdoms caused the history of these two small states to play a significant part in world history. The spirit which emanated from the Hebrew prophets attained heights rarely equaled in the realm of human thought; and for thousands of years the thought and spirit of their work has exerted a strong influence on the history of Europe.

One of the mightiest among the early prophets was Elijah, who lived during the reign of Ahab and Jezebel of the northern kingdom. In protest against the licentious customs of the times, Elijah lived the life of an ascetic in the desert. He journeyed across the land, warning the people against straying from belief in the one God.

The greatest feat reported of him, apart from many legends and fables, is his confrontation with the priests of Baal on Mount Carmel. The Israelites, having settled among the Canaanites had adopted not only their methods of agriculture but in many instances their fertility rites as well. It seemed plausible to them that in order to assure a good harvest they had to sacrifice to the *baalim*—the gods of fertility—on mountain peaks, at springheads, or at trees. They had also adopted the festivals customary at seedtime and during the first and second harvests, whose excessive sensuality and luxury would have been an abomination to Moses and their forefathers in the desert. *JHWH,* they assumed, had no influence on agriculture. When, on Mount Carmel, Elijah successfully pleaded for rain, which the country urgently needed after a long drought, he showed those of little faith that the Lord was also Lord of the rain, Lord of the sowing and reaping.

The prophets continued to inveigh against idol worship and to demand the unconditional return to the Covenant. They not only regarded worship of Baal as idolatry, but also condemned such ceremonial worship of God as was content with offering sacrifices without following God's will and commandments. "I hate, I despise your feasts, and I take no delight in your solemn assemblies," cried the prophet Amos in the name of God. "Even though you offer me your burnt offerings and cereal offerings, I will not accept them. . . . Take away from me the noise of your songs; to the melody of your harps I will not listen. But let justice roll down like waters, and righteousness like an everflowing stream" (Amos 5:21–24).

By "serving God," the prophets meant following the dictates of morality, practicing justice, helping the widows and orphans, loving one's neighbor. "For I desire steadfast love and not sacrifice, the knowledge of God, rather than burnt offerings" (Hosea 6:6). The God who demands this of men is the God not just of Israel. The prophets proclaimed the God of Israel as the *one* God, who is the Lord of all nations.

The prophets concerned themselves not only with religious and moral issues but also with the political trials of their people. Addressing the kings of Israel and Judah, with unparalleled courage and inspired by the wrath of God the prophets reproached them for their greed and violence, their corruption of justice, their senseless seesaw policy between the great powers. In a public speech Jeremiah scourged the despotic King Jehoiakim: " 'But you have eyes and heart only for your dishonest gain, for shedding innocent blood, and for practicing oppression and violence.' Therefore thus says the LORD concerning Jehoiakim the son of Josiah, king of Judah: 'They shall not lament for him. . . . With the burial of an ass he shall be buried, dragged and cast forth beyond the gates of Jerusalem' " (Jeremiah 22:17–19).

The powerful language of the prophets, full of metaphors and poetry, has been faithfully handed down to us, for most of the prophets had disciples who recorded their exhortations and visions.

The Fate of the Southern Kingdom

After the prophets of doom in the northern kingdom had been so amply vindicated by events, the prophet Isaiah became the driving force for internal reforms in Judea, where the descendants of David ruled in uninterrupted succession. The Temple was cleansed of all images of foreign gods. Under King Josiah a further momentous event took place: during the reconstruction of the Temple in Jerusalem in 621 B.C. an ancient scroll was discovered which contained a complete summary of the Mosaic Law—the one we call today the Fifth Book of Moses, or Deuteronomy. The book was read to Josiah and he listened with dismay, for he realized how far his people had strayed from the will of God. He summoned all the elders of Judea to the Temple and, surrounded by priests and prophets, he read the newly discovered book to them and enjoined all those present to observe the commands it contained.

During the reign of Josiah, Assyria was conquered by the Babylonians. When the Assyrian capital of Nineveh fell, the prophets in Jerusalem were jubilant. But Josiah and his weaker successors now became entangled in the struggle between Egypt in the South and the new power of Babylon in the North. After much political turmoil the Babylonians finally conquered Jerusalem. The city and the Temple were destroyed, the king was blinded, his family massacred, and a large part of the population taken as captives to Babylon.

Thus Judea ultimately suffered the same fate as the northern kingdom of Israel. But while Israel remained lost, Judea returned. The exiles settled apart from the rest of the population, avoided any intermingling, and clung to the practice of their faith. This gave them strength and hope. Now the religious reforms and passionate warnings of the prophets bore fruit. In small groups they met in homes to pray, and prayer took the place of sacrifices in the Temple. This was the beginning of what we today call congregations. The special schools built for the prayer assemblies and for reading the Holy Scriptures were the forerunners of synagogues.

The Holy Scriptures now played a decisive role. All extant written tradition was carefully collected and sifted. The importance of the prophets, among whom Ezekiel was the most active during the exile, was now matched by the experts in scriptural exegesis. The yearning for Jerusalem, the destroyed Holy City, always remained alive:

> By the waters of Babylon, there we sat down and
> > wept when we remembered Zion.
> On the willows there
> > we hung up our lyres.
>
> . . . .
>
> How shall we sing the LORD's song in a foreign
> > land?
> If I forget you, O Jerusalem,
> > let my right hand wither!
> > —Psalm 137:1–2, 4–5

After many years of exile, hopes for a return to Zion began to rise anew when Cyrus, the King of the Persians, after victorious campaigns in Asia Minor, prepared for a war against Babylon.

Even before he entered Babylon, the exiles from Judea looked upon him as their future deliverer.

Cyrus fulfilled these hopes; he was magnanimous and, moreover, a Judea settled by grateful repatriates could only be to his advantage. At that time (538–37 B.C.) originated the famous song of rejoicing:

> When the LORD restored the fortunes of Zion,
>> we were like those who dream.
> Then our mouth was filled with laughter,
>> and our tongue with shouts of joy;
> then they said among the nations,
>> "The LORD has done great things for them."
> The LORD had done great things for us;
>> we are glad.
>
> —Psalm 126:1–3

In 537 B.C., after fifty years of exile, fifty thousand Jews started out from Babylon to return across the hostile desert to their homeland.

Renewal of the Covenant Under Ezra

The repatriates found a desolated land. But they had hardly settled down when they began to rebuild God's Temple in Jerusalem; it was consecrated in 516 B.C. The King's governor in Judea at that time was Zerubbabel, a descendant of the old royal house. However, the return to power of David's dynasty came to nought because of the opposition of both the Persian rulers and the priests who insisted on a religious leader as head of the new Judea. Henceforth the high priest of Jerusalem took the place of the king.

Loyalty to the land of their fathers was so great among the Jews that in the following hundred years groups of pilgrims again and again made their way back from Babylon. Among their leaders were men who had been appointed to high office at the Babylonian court. One of them was Ezra, a royal scribe. The first to summon the "great assembly," the Sanhedrin, he made the Law of Moses, the entire Torah, the binding law for all those who had returned from exile. In order to insure compliance he waged a successful campaign against marriages with alien women. In 444 B.C., shortly before the beginning of the autumnal harvest festival, the people assembled in Jerusalem to pledge themselves to a renewal of the Covenant. For many hours Ezra himself read and expounded the Torah to the people who stood before him in reverent silence. He recalled for them how they were to celebrate the "Feast of the Harvest." He reminded them to build tents or booths in remembrance of the time when their fathers lived in the desert and received the Torah.

From this time on, the hallowing of the Sabbath also became one of the foremost duties of pious Jews. The recurrent day of rest, now a universally accepted custom, is a gift of Israel to mankind. According to the book of Genesis, "And there was evening and there was morning, one day" (Genesis 1:5b). The Sabbath begins on Friday night at sunset and ends Saturday at darkness. All work is strictly forbidden on the Sabbath, so that even the meals have to be cooked the day before and kept warm. On the Sabbath domestic animals and servants are also bidden to rest. Among permissible activities are reading the Scriptures and visiting the sick.

This New Covenant with God underwent its most severe test when Judea was forcibly drawn into the sphere of Greek culture, whose influence rapidly spread throughout the then-known world in the wake of the conquests of Alexander the Great. In Judea, too, there were quite a number of "Hellenists," who willingly succumbed to the allure of Greek culture and philosophy. But there were also the "Hasidim," the pious ones, who clung to the faith of their fathers. Their resistance was aroused when the Syrian ruler Antiochus IV began forcibly to hellenize the country he ruled. He banned the Jewish rites, demanded that the Greek deities be worshiped, and had a statue of Zeus erected in the Temple. His mercenaries amused themselves by forcing the pious Jews to eat the forbidden pork. Here for the first time in history we encounter martyrdom—putting infinite loyalty to God above the suffering of torture and death.

This forcible hellenization also aroused a spirit of militancy. The pious patriots gathered around the priest Mattathias and his five sons, hid in isolated mountain areas until they had grown into an army, and then began their holy war. They were led by

Mattathias' third son, Judah, who was given the name Maccabee, meaning "hammer." Judah and his men fought with unequaled courage against the Syrians, who often outnumbered them. Finally they succeeded in obtaining a guarantee of religious freedom for the Jewish people. The Temple in Jerusalem was consecrated anew, and in memory of this event the Jews to this day celebrate Chanukah, lighting the eight-armed candelabra.

Eventually, Judah's youngest brother, Simon, became high priest, prince, and field marshal, and founded a new dynasty, the Hasmoneans. The Jews, now in full control of their country, were faced with a new problem as regards the non-Jews in their midst. What rights were to be accorded the minority groups? Was the law of the land, both civil and religious, to be one and the same for everyone? A choice had to be made between imposing religious conformity and permitting religious diversity. It was decided that civil law was binding upon everyone, that is, prohibitions of murder, theft, cruelty to animals, sexual license, blasphemy, and so forth, but that the ceremonial laws of Judaism were to apply to Jews only. Beyond the prohibitions of civil law, non-Jews were free to follow the dictates of their own religious beliefs or irreligious inclinations. Unfortunately under the Hasmonean dynasty, forced conversions of aliens to Judaism occurred, and when the Pharisees protested there was a terrible conflict. It is an irony of history that the Jews, who were to spend the next two thousand years in the shadow of religious persecution, were the very people who formulated the ideal of religious diversity and made it the law of the land at a time when they had the upper hand.

For about seventy-five years Judea maintained its independence. But then the descendants of the Hasmoneans began to quarrel over succession. Eventually Herodes, an outsider, seized power by having himself appointed by the new world power, Rome, as tribute-paying King of Judea. He was a capable and energetic, but cruel ruler. Above all, he was jealous of his children by one of his wives, the Hasmonean Mariamne. He had this entire family massacred, and distributed the land among his remaining sons by other wives. Thus weakened, the country came increasingly under Roman rule. Utlimately, Rome proceeded to appoint procurators or governors, who collected taxes and administered the country.

2

Hopes for a Messiah and Jesus of Nazareth

The Prophets' Hopes for a Messiah

While the storms of history raged over the small land of Judea, the scribes continued to sift and collect the books of the Law, the testimony of the prophets, and the songs and proverbs. At that time a new kind of collection was begun, called the Greek *apocalypses,* or "revelations." They contained visions of the future of mankind, especially of the end of days, which was thought to be imminent. Of these often-confused and enigmatic writings, only the Book of Daniel was accepted into the Jewish canon of the Holy Scriptures.

At that time the question of the future concerned people in a way which we can hardly imagine today. In those days many Jews believed that the just would be resurrected, while the evil would be condemned to eternal death. The belief that evil would be punished in hell and righteousness rewarded in heaven came only later.

Of much more significance, however, was the hope for a future deliverer, a Messiah (*Moschiach* in Hebrew, meaning "Anointed One"). This hope originated with the prophets, in particular with Isaiah, Zechariah, and Ezekiel. The concept of the Messiah was not always the same. In the sayings of some of the prophets, he was described as a warlike hero, a king of the tribe of David, who would destroy the godless and establish a kingdom of power and glory. Others saw him as a servant of God, poor, despised, and wretched, who would take upon himself the sins of his people

31

and thus bring about their salvation and deliverance, not by force but by the spirit.

Closely tied to the hope for a Messiah was the concept of a Day of Divine Judgment. The more oppression and violence the believers had to suffer, the more fervently they believed that this day was at hand. They prepared themselves by atonement and meditation for the Day of Judgment, on which God would appear in his glory. Shortly before this day, the prophet Malachi had foretold, the prophet Elijah would return and turn the hearts of the children to their fathers. Not only oppression and terror, but also signs and miracles would herald the approaching end of days. Once the deliverance was accomplished, the Messiah would return on the clouds of heaven, in divine glory, as the "Son of Man"—the strange and awesome term used in the Book of Daniel. All these prophetic visions were alive among the people, and expectations ran high whenever suffering and oppression were felt. This was the case when Pontius Pilate was the Roman procurator. His regime was cruel and arbitrary, and repeatedly he tried to force the Jews to accept the hated cult of the Caesars. Thus when *Jehoshua* ("Jesus") of Nazareth began to preach in the synagogues of Galilee and Judea, and emphatically announced that the time was fast approaching, the tormented people began to listen and to wonder, as so often before, whether he were the Elijah who was awaited as the harbinger of the Messiah. The disciples who gathered around the eloquent preacher also at first regarded him as this herald.

Another preacher, too, by the name of *Jochanan* ("John"), in those years called the people to atonement in the deserts on the Jordan and made his followers undergo a ritual immersion as a confirmation of their repentance. He sent a messenger to ask Jesus whether he were the one who was to come. Jesus had word sent to him that the time had progressed further, signs and miracles were occurring, the sick were being healed and the devil driven out, and that—if he could grasp the fact—he, John himself, was the Elijah. Thus he hinted at the secret that he announced only on a few occasions, that he knew himself to be the Messiah, the one whose suffering would bring the deliverance, as the prophets had proclaimed. On Mount Tabor, for the first time, he revealed himself as the Messiah to his three most trusted apostles, Peter, James, and John. They were deeply moved by this revelation and thought they were seeing Jesus together with Moses and Elijah. Later, while they were at Caesarea Philippi, all the apostles learned the secret, for to the question "But who do you say I am?" Peter now replied, "You are the Christ," meaning "You are the Messiah." ("Christ" is the literal Greek translation of the word *Messiah*.) "Then he strictly charged the disciples to tell no one that he was Christ." But of the sufferings and oppression that were yet to come, Jesus spoke again and again.

Jesus' Trial and Death

Fully conscious of the martyrdom that he would have to suffer, but at the same time firmly convinced that the secret of his being the Messiah would be revealed when he returned as the "Son of Man" in the clouds of heaven, Jesus went up to Jerusalem with his disciples at the time of Passover. At this time Jerusalem was crowded with pilgrims from all over the country who had come to sacrifice the Passover lamb in the Temple. Large crowds gave Jesus a festive welcome, taking him to be the herald of the expected Messiah. The secular and spiritual authorities had every reason to be watchful during the holidays, since the pilgrims' feasts had often given rise to religious and political unrest. For this reason the Roman procurator changed his residence from Caesarea to Jerusalem to be able to intervene instantly if the necessity arose.

Here it was that one of the disciples betrayed the secret that Jesus was the Messiah—which they had all been pledged not to reveal—to the Sanhedrin, the spiritual authority of Judea. Enormous hopes were attached to the appearance of the Messiah; moreover, there had at various times been several others who had claimed to be Messiah. Hence it was not surprising that the High Council regarded this news as extremely dangerous and sacrilegious. Jesus was arrested and led before the High Council. To the question "Are you the Messiah?" he replied, "I am he." This ended the hearing; there was no need for the examination of any other witness, for Jesus himself had affirmed the crucial count of the indictment, fully conscious of what the consequences must be. He was ready to take upon himself the sufferings through which alone, according to the Scriptures, the Messiah could bring about the salvation and enter into his glory.

As was the custom then, the hearing before the spiritual authorities was followed by a trial before the Roman procurator. Understandably enough, Pilate was more interested in the worldly aspects of the hopes for the coming of the Messiah. He knew that a large part of the Jewish people hoped to find in the Messiah a king who would deliver them from the Roman yoke. Hence he asked, "Are you the King of the Jews?" and again Jesus answered with only a few words: "You have said so" (Matthew 27:11). In the meantime some pilgrims had gathered around the palace to condemn him.

Sentence of death was pronounced, and it was carried out by the Roman soldiers in the cruel form of crucifixion, then customary among the Romans. Among the words of the dying Jesus handed down to us is one which asks God's forgiveness for all those who were the instruments of his death, "Father, forgive them; for they know not what they do" (Luke 23:34).

The Hope for Jesus' Return

During those days of terror the disciples had dispersed like a flock without its shepherd. But they came together again and remembered the words spoken by their Master at their Last Supper: that he would return and walk before them to Galilee. They found his grave empty; it also occurred to them more than once that they saw him bodily among them and as in former times heard him speak to them and instruct them. This filled them with the certain belief that their Master had been raised from the dead and that this was the first step toward the expected deliverance; the second would be his return in the clouds of heaven, at the right side of God.

They proclaimed this belief and baptized everyone willing to accept the crucified one as the Messiah. They continued to preach repentance and a pious life, to share everything they had, and to wait for the ". . . times of refreshing [that] may come from the presence of the Lord, and that he may send the Christ appointed for you, Jesus" (Acts 3:19b–20).

Both Jews and Christians hoped for an early coming of the end of days—for the deliverance. The apostles lived in the certainty that the Day of Judgment would come before they themselves tasted death. These hopes differed only in one point: *The Jews were expecting a Messiah, whose face they did not yet know. The Christians expected to see in the coming redeemer the crucified Jesus of Nazareth.*

And so it is to this day. As Jesus has not returned and the messianic hopes of the Jews have not been fulfilled, both Jews and Christians are still waiting for the day of God.

But soon the Apostle Paul carried the interpretation of the life of Jesus a step further. He taught that through faith in the crucified and resurrected Christ the sinner could become a new man and partake of eternal life. By having faith, and being sustained by baptism and communion, the Christian could suffer and be resurrected with his Lord. Moreover, Paul taught that Christ was the essence of the Law and that justice could be attained by faith in him. This proved to be decisive in bringing the faith to the "nations," that is, to the non-Jews. At a council in Jerusalem, Paul convinced the disciples that the communities in Asia Minor and the rest of the world that had been converted so successfully should not conform to the ritual demands of the Torah. Equally important for the future was Paul's concept of the person of Jesus. He had not known Jesus himself. For him, Jesus the man and the servant of God became transfigured into an emissary of heaven, who dwelled only briefly among men and then returned to heaven. The doctrine of Christ as God's Son, which later led to the doctrine of the Trinity, was in the eyes of the Jews a deviation from the meaning of the first commandment: that the Lord alone is God. But for the people in the Greco-Roman civilization this doctrine evoked familiar concepts of the sons of gods who came down to earth to perform miraculous deeds.

Thus Paul prepared the ground in the first Christian communities for the later dissemination of this faith. In the meantime, world history marched on, the struggle of the Jews against the Roman yoke continued, and the chronicles of the time took no note of the small new sect that had been founded among the people of Judea.

3

The Destruction of Jerusalem and the Revolt of Bar-Kochba

Sadducees, Pharisees, and Essenes

During the period of independence which the small Jewish state enjoyed under the first Hasmonean king, two political trends had evolved which were to play a significant role in the country's further development.

The party of the Sadducees was an aristocratic-priestly party. For them the center of the nation was the Temple with its sacrificial service. But like all other nations, Israel was to engage in power politics and, if necessary, resort to war. The Sadducees stood firmly by the Torah, but were not interested in a wider development and application of its "instructions." They were, moreover, of the opinion that strict observance of the law was primarily the duty of the priests, but not of the people as a whole.

The Pharisees, on the other hand, were a democratic-synagogal party. They based their argument on the Mosaic commandment "You shall be a holy people unto Me." Hence they demanded that all Jews strictly observe the instructions of the Torah. Their goal was not secular and political power, but the setting apart of the Jewish people as a consecrated and spiritual nation centered around the teachings of God and loyalty to his Covenant with them. This is conveyed by the name "Pharisees," which derives from the

36

Hebrew *Peruschim*—"those set apart." The hub of their activities was the house of learning, the synagogues of the land, not the Temple. As long as the Jews could live according to the Law of their forefathers, the Pharisees were a peace-loving party. They expected salvation, not from conquest but as a result of acts of religious purity. The Pharisees were profoundly serious about the strict observance of the Law. Quite incorrectly, "Pharisee" has come to connote in modern times the hypocrite and the self-righteous. Naturally, such deviations—inevitable whenever high demands are made on men—occurred among the Pharisees. Jesus had already criticized the danger of merely external observance of the Law, as did the Pharisees themselves. But one must not underestimate the great spiritual conviction of this movement.

The passionate zeal of the Pharisees always came to the fore when the religious constitution seemed to be in danger. Then, the zealots among them were ready to take up arms, oblivious of all risks. They were prepared to make the greatest sacrifices, not for worldly or political goals, but for their religion.

Both movements were concerned with the existence of the Jewish people among the nations. Opposed to both was a third, smaller group, the Essenes; who were not interested in questions of nation and state. To them, becoming holy and pure was a means for personal deliverance, not for the "conservation of the people." Hence the Essenes lived according to far stricter rules than did the Pharisees. Much like a monastic order—though not bound to celibacy—they retreated to the rocks and deserts near the Dead Sea. None of them were allowed to possess personal property. Their way of life was very simple. They rejected Temple sacrifices and, instead, ate their meals together as a communal sacrifice, thanking God for his gifts. Very often, not only during the day, but also at night, immersions were prescribed for external and internal purification. Most probably, John the Baptist was close to this sect. Many customs of the Essenes were later adopted by the early Christian communities.

The Destruction of the Temple

The Hasmonean kings sometimes stood under the influence of the Sadducees, while at other times they were influenced by the Pharisees. Under Roman rule, however, these movements were of secondary importance, since political independence and religious autonomy were equally stifled. The people in the provinces were so oppressed by taxation and abuses of every kind that small Judea soon became a critical focus of unrest in the Roman Empire. There are records of a number of uprisings, especially during the time of the Roman procurators. At that time a terrorist group sprang up among the zealots—the "Dagger Men" (*Sicarians*)—who wanted to bring things to a head by violence. They made many attempts to assassinate not only Romans, but also collaborators among their own people. Occasionally these groups grew into regular partisan units. In A.D. 66 the zealots together with the Sicarians succeeded in starting an open revolt in Jerusalem and defeated the Syrian governor, who had led an army against them. Thereupon the Roman troops under the procurator Florus in Caesarea committed a barbaric act of vengeance: They massacred the entire Jewish community of Caesarea, consisting of many thousands of people.

This blood bath further inflamed the wrath of the insurgent Jews. Everywhere they took up arms for a war of national liberation. They appointed Joseph ben Mattathias, a scribe, as supreme commander of Galilee. He had lived for two years in Rome and had been deeply impressed by Rome's political and administrative genius. Although the mismanagement of the Roman governors in Judea enraged him, he was convinced that an open rebellion against Rome was ultimately doomed to failure and could only worsen the position of his people.

Emperor Nero dispatched Flavius Vespasianus to put down the revolt. He arrived in Syria with his son Titus and advanced with his main army against Galilee. He met with little resistance in the open country, as Joseph ben Mattathias (also "Flavius Josephus") had retired to the fortress of Jotapata, which he defended for a month and a half.

We are indebted to Josephus for a record of these events, because after Jotapata was conquered, he let himself be taken prisoner under rather ignoble circumstances and offered Vespasianus his services. The fact that he adopted the additional name "Flavius" is one evidence of his admiration for the Romans. As adviser to Vespasianus and Titus he participated in the campaign and later wrote *Jewish Antiquities,* the most important source for Jewish history of that period.

Soon after, Vespasianus was proclaimed Emperor in Rome. He returned to Rome and left Titus to lay siege to and conquer Jerusalem. Led by the zealots, the defenders of the capital put up a heroic resistance, which will remain forever memorable. They were finally overpowered by Rome's highly developed battering rams and catapults, and by hunger. At the beginning of the siege large stores of food had caught fire. When, exhausted by hunger, the defenders secretly tried to leave the city in order to obtain food, they were caught by Titus' men and crucified by the hundreds in front of the city walls or sent back with their hands cut off. Such cruelties spurred rather than broke the resistance of the defenders. Finally, Titus decided to starve them out. He had ramparts erected around the city and manned with guards so that not a single inhabitant could escape. What now took place within the encircled city was heart-breaking. Hunger drove some to insanity: they fought over every scrap of garbage, over hay and bits of leather. Others, completely exhausted and numbed, looked for death to come.

Titus then proceeded to storm the mount on which the Temple stood. Flavius Josephus, who was with the besieging force outside the city tried several times to persuade the garrison to capitulate, but in vain. Finally, the defenders were pushed back into the Temple proper. In the Roman camp a debate was in progress as to whether the edifice should be spared, since it was world renowned, or destroyed, in order to "crush the obstinate Jews." The first view prevailed, but when the final, bitter battle began, the Roman soldiers threw burning torches into the Temple square, which soon became a sea of flames. A terrible panic broke out. Josephus wrote later: "Hidden in flames, the Temple hill seemed to burn from within; but the rivers of blood ran even faster than the torrents of fire . . . the ground was covered with corpses; the soldiers climbed over mounds of bodies in pursuit of the fleeing garrison."

At the end of the five-months siege there remained only a smouldering heap of ruins where once had stood the high-towered city whose name meant "Place of Peace." Of the walls of the fortress only a small part remained, the famous Wailing Wall, at which, centuries later, pious Jewish pilgrims were to lament the loss of the Temple. Only a few prisoners were released; most of them were sold into slavery or driven to their deaths in gladiatorial games. Those leaders of the defenders who remained alive were taken to Rome as prisoners, together with the relics of the Temple that had been saved from the flames. They were paraded in the triumphal march which is immortalized on the Arch of Titus in Rome.

The Origin of the Patriarchate and the Revolt of Bar-Kochba

For Jewish history the destruction of the Temple and the prohibition against rebuilding it had two important consequences: The ground was cut from under the party of Sadducees, and the Jewish people henceforward followed solely the path of the Pharisees, the way of spiritual communion—rebirth by way of religious observance. Since the destruction of the Temple had also put an end to the daily sacrificial services, the word—the teachings—became the core of the Jewish religion.

The place of the kings and high priests was taken by scholar-teachers. A Jewish history recounts that a few days before the fall of Jerusalem the most eminent scholar of his time, Jochanan ben Zakai, had escaped from the city, hidden in a coffin, and that Titus had allowed him and a few of his pupils to reside in the city of Jabne. Legend or not, the fact is that Jabne became the center of a spiritual renaissance. The High Council consisted of scholars and was headed by a patriarch, whom the Romans too acknowledged as the representative of the Jewish people. The office of the patriarch became hereditary and continued for over three hundred years. There were few other political changes. The country, still settled largely by Jews, continued to be ruled by a Roman governor.

However, the rebellious spirit had not yet been extinguished. In A.D. 115 there were sudden uprisings in the Jewish communities outside Palestine—in Mesopotamia, in Egypt, and in Cyprus. They could only be suppressed by the most cruel measures. In Palestine, too, resistance against the Roman rule flamed up anew in A.D. 132. The leader of this revolt, which initially was successful, was Simon Bar-Kozeba, who was called *Bar-Kochba,* that is, "Son of a Star." The name conveys the great force that radiated from this man. The rebels, who had succeeded in occupying Jerusalem, remained victorious for three years. Then Emperor Hadrian set the Roman war machine in motion and their fate was sealed. Bar-Kochba fell in battle. The most outstanding Jewish scholar of the time, Rabbi Akiba, was captured and flayed alive with iron combs in the public place of execution, while unto his last breath he recited the ancient Jewish prayer: "Hear, O Israel: The LORD our God is one LORD; and you shall love the LORD your God with all your heart, and with all your soul, and with all your might" (Deuteronomy 6:4–5). In coming centuries untold numbers of Jewish martyrs were to die with this prayer on their lips.

Jerusalem was now called "Aelia Capitolina" by the Romans. Jews were forbidden to enter the city. The name "Judea" vanished from the chronicles and was replaced by "Syria palaestina." A wave of religious persecution began which, however, had so little success that soon the Jews were again permitted to practice their religion.

4

Synagogue, Church, and State

The Significance of the Diaspora

The fact that for almost six hundred years large Jewish communities had existed, not only in Palestine but also in many places of the world then known, was becoming increasingly significant. The dispersion of the Jews (*diaspora* in Greek; *galuth* in Hebrew) had had its beginning in the Babylonian exile. Since then Babylon had had a large Jewish colony, for not all the captives had returned. Almost at the same time a sizable Jewish military settlement had come into existence in Egypt when the Pharaohs assumed the protectorate over Judea. This colony, in the neighborhood of what today is Aswan, had even built its own Temple. During Persia's rule of Palestine many Jews were drawn to the Persian court. The Book of Esther—even though highly embellished—tells their story. To this day the Purim Festival is observed in grateful remembrance of the rescue of the Jews from the vicious plot of Haman, the royal chamberlain, through the intercession of the Jewish Queen, Esther. It is celebrated in joyful exuberance by masked processions.

For a time the Jewish community of Alexandria achieved particular eminence. Here Jewish scholars translated the five books of Moses into Greek, thereby preparing the way for Judaism's influence on the Greco-Roman world. The sublime account of the creation, the tremendous moral force of the biblical commandments, and the spiritual effect of the *one* demanding God attracted many who had begun to question the all-too-human Olympic gods.

42

Judaism at that time had many sympathizers as well as converts. This led to the growth of the Jewish communities in some of the towns and cities in Asia Minor and Greece that had been originally established as trading colonies or settlements by freed slaves. There were now flourishing Jewish communities in Ephesus, Miletus, and Pergamon, in Athens, Corinth, and Philippi, as well as in Rome. They became the base of the Apostle Paul's missionary activities. When, after the fall of Jerusalem and the revolt of Bar-Kochba, many Jews were sold into slavery, the communities of the diaspora tried to free as many of their co-religionists as possible.

The Teachings of the Torah Become Anchored in the Talmud

The external defeat now led the Jews to concentrate on a spiritual task that was to become fundamental for the future: the development of the Talmud. For some time there had existed, side by side with the twenty-four books of the Hebrew Bible acknowledged as binding (canonized), a rich oral tradition. It comprised the sayings of the great teachers (rabbis) and their interpretations of the Torah. The rabbis, the eminent interpreters of the Torah, henceforward became the national ideal. Rabbis did not have to be either consecrated or descended from a priestly family. A saying of the time was "There are three crowns: the crown of the Torah, the crown of the priesthood, the crown of the royalty. . . . The crown of the Torah is within the reach of everyone, and whoever has acquired it stands before God as if the three crowns had lain before him and he had acquired them all." Anyone could become a rabbi if he zealously studied the Torah and had God-given wisdom. These masters of the Word of God usually earned their livelihood at common occupations.

One of the most beloved of these teachers was Hillel the Elder, who lived from 75 B.C. to A.D. 5. He had come to Judea from the diaspora in Babylon and was soon elected head of the Sanhedrin. He was a master at merging respect for the authority of the Scriptures with the requirements of everyday life. To answer a questioner he turned the ancient biblical commandment ". . . you shall love your neighbor as yourself . . ." (Leviticus 19:18) into the telling version, "What is hateful to you, don't do to your neighbor. That is the basic content of the Torah; everything else is commentary thereon." Other memorable sayings of Hillel: "A name made great is a name destroyed; he who does not increase his knowledge, decreases it; and he who does not study deserves to die . . . ." "If I am not for myself, who will be for me? And if I am only for myself, what am I? And if [I do] not [do] now [what has to be done], when [will I do it]?" Again and again we find evidence of Hillel's wisdom, benevolence, and inexhaustible patience.

The orally transmitted sayings and interpretations were called the *Mishna* (*shana,* meaning "to learn," "to repeat"). By A.D. 200 these oral traditions had been assembled, edited, and recorded in Palestine in order to permit uniform interpretation of Scripture. The Mishna is divided into six main parts:

1. The laws concerning prayers, agriculture, tithes, and offerings to priests.

2. The festivals of the Jewish year.

3. Laws concerning marriage and the family.

4. Civil and criminal law.

5. Temple ritual and laws concerning humane slaughter and food.

6. Ritual uncleanliness.

But this did not include the task of collection and sifting. Numerous exegeses and critical discussions—commentaries, as we would call them—were added to the Mishna. Called *Gemara,* they were the record of the religio-legal debates which took place in the houses of learning in Palestine and Babylon. The debates were conducted with a display of much learnedness and acuity, but also with a delight in highly technical theological differentiation. Hence these commentaries ramble on and on; history mixes with legend, parables with proverbs. They also contain a variety of medical advice, astronomy, and other scientific information, which the disputants thought worthy to offer.

This tremendous collection, Mishna plus Gemara, came to be called the *Talmud* (from *lamad,* meaning "to learn"). There are two editions of the Talmud, the Palestinian and the Babylonian; the latter was finished about a hundred years later and is three times larger than the Palestinian. In an English translation (*Soncino*) the Talmud comprises seventeen volumes, each having hundreds of pages.

This singular and highly diversified cultural document is obviously anything but easy to read. Generations of Jews in the diaspora were later schooled with its help. It made heavy demands on the intelligence and the powers of concentration. Difficult as it is to penetrate the opaque whole of this work, it is easy to take isolated sentences out of context and to use them against the Jews. Unfortunately, this method has been used to our day and has led to grievous misunderstandings regarding the essence of the Talmud.

Jews and Christians in the Roman Empire

While Jewish houses of learning were thus collecting intellectual ammunition for future use, the Jews were also increasingly faced with the necessity of theological debates with the growing Christian communities. The Christians regarded the destruction of the Temple as a confirmation of their faith, as a divine judgement on the "stiff-necked Jews," who would not acknowledge their Messiah. This argument could also prove to the pagans that God had turned his "back" on the Jews and that henceforward the Christians were the new "People of the Covenant." This claim was based on a far-reaching theological decision. There had been tendencies in some Christian communities to cast out the entire Old Testament as being a Jewish book and to accept only the Gospels and Epistles. But the majority of bishops and church fathers had rejected this demand as erroneous. In their opinion the entire Old Testament pointed clearly to Jesus as the Messiah. "The Old Testament," said St. Augustine, "is but the New Testament covered with a veil, and the New Testament but the Old Testament revealed."

This decision was doubly important: For the Jews it was bound to be unjust and painful. Their Holy Book had been, so to speak, torn from them, and in the hands of Christian interpreters it was being used as an intellectual arsenal against Judaism. Yet on the other hand this very emphasis preserved the historical and spiritual connection between Judaism and Christianity. For Christianity a separation from the Old Testament would have been tantamount to cutting off its own roots. The joint possession of the Old Testament established an indissoluble bond between the two faiths.

The dispute between the mother and the daughter religion grew quite sharp as early as the first three decades, but only spiritual weapons, that is, theological arguments, were used. Nearly all the church fathers battled with the Jews and their "obduracy." They thought that it was only out of ill will that the Jews refused to acknowledge Jesus as the Messiah. They ignored the fact that on their part the Jews had good reason to point out that Jesus had not rebuilt the Kingdom of David, nor had he brought about the Kingdom of God, which in their view and that of the prophets was to have been more than an "inner experience."

Vis-à-vis paganism, Jews and Christians were united in rejecting the pagan pantheon and in refusing to pay religious tribute to the Roman Emperor. The pagans regarded Christianity as simply a modified form of Judaism. Even after the insurrection of A.D. 132, Judaism was permitted to continue as a religious community, while Christianity was often regarded as a dangerous secret cult which had to be repressed. There were isolated incidents of Christians being persecuted as early as the first and second century, and under the emperors Decius and Diocletian in the third and fourth centuries persecution became systematic. The church father Tertullian said at that time: "Christians are being blamed for every mishap befalling the state and for every misfortune suffered by the people. Whenever the Tiber floods its banks or the Nile fails to irrigate its fields, whenever the sky is without rain or the earth quakes, whenever there is famine or a plague, the cry is raised: 'Throw the Christians to the lions!'" The Christians could now vie with the Jews in loyalty to their faith and bear testimony to it through martyrdom. In this respect, too, Tertullian was right in saying, "The blood of the martyrs is the seed of the Church." Persecution furthered rather than hindered the propagation of the new faith.

The Church and the Synagogue

When in A.D. 312 the Emperor Constantine defeated his adversary Maxentios, the part played by the Christian communities in the disintegrating Roman Empire had become so important that Constantine attributed his victory to the God of the Christians and became a convert. Soon thereafter he proclaimed Christianity the official religion. This proclamation brought about a basic change in the relationship between the church and the synagogue. The church had become victorious. Those recently persecuted now had the power to persecute in turn. A great number were superficially converted, and joined the church. They confirmed their membership by taking part in the sacraments, which they probably considered to have a particularly efficacious and magical content. Increasingly the sacraments became the focus of the rapidly growing church. They assured the Christian of salvation and, at the same time, protected him from the devil and the demons. It then followed that every person who remained outside the sacramental community was considered the prey of the powers of hell—someone through whom Satan could realize his evil intent. This fear of the devil was directed particularly against the Jews, who were soon also suspected of practicing anti-Christian magic. This was the basis for equating the Jews with the devil, which throughout the Middle Ages led to numerous bloody persecutions.

One must not, however, imagine that this superstitious fear of the Jews existed from the beginning. Actually, it was to a large extent the result of the measures which the victorious church employed against the synagogue. These measures were often adopted because Christians by no means kept themselves as isolated from the Jews as their bishops would have wished; in fact, the synagogue, and particularly the Jewish holidays, exerted a certain attraction for Christians.

One of the first laws which the church promulgated, in A.D. 325, was to separate the Christian feast of Easter from the Jewish holiday of Passover. The Christians were also constrained not to observe their day of rest in common with the Jews. They were to keep only Sunday, the day of Christ's resurrection, hallowed. The church father John Chrysostom, a powerful orator, had occasion to inveigh against Christians who allowed themselves to be seduced by Jewish customs: "Among the miserable and wretched Jews a number of Holy Days are presently being celebrated. There is the sound of the ram horns, there are the leafy tabernacles and days of fasting. Many of our people go there to gape at the ceremonies and some do not scruple to take part in the festivities and the fasting! . . . I know only too well that many feel respect toward the Jews and consider their ceremonies to be holy. I am, therefore, determined to tear out this pernicious attitude by the roots." Chrysostom admitted that there were no idols in the synagogues, but stated that "The demons feel all the more at home there." Christian men were not to let their women go there because they would "return with the devil in their souls."

This sermon is an example of how the church now set itself against the Jews more resolutely than ever before. The argument was used, "You are unlucky; therefore you are in the wrong. We are successful; therefore right is on our side." Such thinking was all the more dangerous, as the church was now closely allied with the power of the state. Thus the dispute between the church and the synagogue shifted from the religious to the legal plane.

The Jews and the Empire

Emperor Constantine considered his regime to be the earthly image of God's reign in heaven. The question which had played such an important part in early Jewish history—How is the dominion of God to be realized on earth?—now arose again in regard to Christian authority over a Christian state. The contradictions inherent in this issue revealed themselves in many different ways during the succeeding centuries, and have not been completely resolved to this day.

Constantine and his successors, however, tackled the difficult task posed by this question and did not hesitate to buttress their theological convictions with legal means. In their opinion, only those could be first-class citizens of a Christian state who also partook of the Christian sacraments. Jews, heretics, and pagans were therefore excluded from certain civic rights. It was also thought to be inconceivable for Christians to be subordinate to Jews. Jews

were therefore prevented from entering the military and administrative services. For the same reason they were forbidden to own
Christian slaves, "as we consider it unjust that pious servants be
sullied by being owned by Godless masters." Later the Jews were
also prohibited from owning pagan slaves. This prohibition had
far-reaching consequences as it made it very difficult, if not impossible, for Jews to engage in agriculture as it was then practiced.

In the sixth century Emperor Justinian made these legal restrictions even more rigorous and incorporated them in the *corpus
juris civilis,* the great legal system which he had ordered drawn up
and which exerted a lasting influence on the legal systems of the
western world.

The Jews were thus defined by law as aliens. In later times the
German emperors of the Holy Roman Empire extended a special
protective guardianship over the Jews. Charlemagne recognized
that the Jews could be of great service to him as merchants,
traders, and interpreters. They owned trading posts in all the cities
of Europe and the Near East where Jewish communities existed.
Thus they were in an excellent position to engage in international
trade with spices, precious cloth, rare metals, and frankincense.
But they were also useful in diplomatic missions, where their extensive knowledge of languages was of great value. Charlemagne
sent a Jew by the name of Isaac to the court of the renowned
Caliph Haroun-al-Rashid. He returned to Aix-la-Chapelle with an
elephant as a gift from the Caliph to the Emperor.

Under Charlemagne's son, Louis the Pious, so-called Imperial
letters of protection were issued to individual Jews or Jewish communities. Jews who enjoyed such protection were not to be
harassed or maligned. Their property was not to be touched, nor
were they to be forced to render special tributes. They were permitted to buy non-Christian slaves and their testimony before a
court of law carried the same weight as that of a Christian. Louis's
noble attitude is confirmed in a handwritten annotation, which he
made in the margin of an ordinance which permitted some Jews
to own land: "Although apostolic doctrine obliges us to practice
charity only towards those professing the faith, it by no means
forbids us to be charitable towards those outside the faith. In truth,

it urges us to emulate God's mercy and make no distinction between believers and non-believers."

The Saxon emperors, too, continued this benevolent policy. However, during the time of the Crusades this protection became the so-called *servitudo camerae,* which meant "pay as you [are permitted to] live." The Jews were now regarded as "slaves of the Crown," as bondsmen of the Imperial Chamber. In return for Imperial protection, which often was of little value, they had to pay considerable amounts of money. Every time a new emperor began his reign protection had to be sought—and paid for—anew. Not infrequently the Emperor farmed out these lucrative sources of income to territorial princes or to cities, who in turn raised the amount of the tribute in order to line their own pockets. When a Jew died without heirs, his property went to the Emperor. The combination of protection on the one hand and tribute on the other opened the door for gross abuses.

The Jews and the Papacy

Until the Crusades there were repeated examples of the clergy inveighing against friendly and neighborly relations between the Jews and Christians. The popes, too, in the interest of doctrinal purity, strongly advocated segregation. As a rule, however, they disapproved of the destruction of synagogues and of other excesses, which frequently occurred under the leadership of fanatical members of the lower clergy. Among these were in particular the "forced baptisms," which many Christians again and again were tempted to commit because they mistakenly attributed magic properties to the sacrament. Ugly incidents of this kind occurred especially during the seventh century in Spain. Here even bishops instigated assaults on synagogues. In long-winded missives to other bishops they boasted specifically of the forced baptisms that had been performed. The highest church authorities, however, considered forced conversions undesirable, not only because, according to the Apostle Paul in his Epistle to the Romans, God has not revoked his promise to the people of Israel, but also because force is more likely to create bitterness than loyalty. According to the doctrine of the church, Christ would only return when the Jews recognized Jesus as their Messiah, which, of course, presumed their voluntary conversion.

The position adopted by the popes did not prevent the continuation of enforced baptisms. The fact that most of the popes opposed the crude and superstitious accusations against the Jews which later gained currency also did not prevent these superstitions from resulting in grievous suffering for the Jews.

One of the papal decrees, however, was to prove directly disastrous to the Jews, although it was not directed at them at all. It was intended for the Christians, who were now forbidden to collect interest. Reference was made to Moses and the Fifteenth Psalm. The church understood usury to mean not only excessive interest (as it does today), but anything that exceeded the simple repayment of the principal of a loan. At times even merchants were called usurers, as they had to sell more dearly than they had bought.

These rigid law-givers had little understanding of economic processes. But then, as now, it was necessary to finance large undertakings in advance; for example, merchant ships were built which would bring a profit only at some later date. The princes in particular were constantly in need of money for their wars, which they could only repay after having looted the enemy. It was therefore impossible to manage without cash capital, and any person of common sense realized that the lender had to be compensated for his loan and the risk he incurred by payment of interest. The Jews, however, were the only citizens to whom the strictures of the church did not apply. Inevitably, they therefore assumed the indispensable function of money-lending because they were given no alternative.

As a result Christians now became indebted to the Jews and the term *usurer* was equated with *Jew*. Religious segregation was accompanied by economic envy and the not unusual hatred of debtors for their creditors. This was to have horrible consequences for the Jews.

5

The Jews and Islam

Mohammed's New Religion

In the year A.D. 570 Mohammed was born in Mecca. In a cave not far from his birthplace he had visions that called him to be the prophet of the Arabs. Unable to read, he knew the tales of the Old Testament and the Talmud from hearsay and was also acquainted with popular versions of the New Testament and the stories of the saints. This knowledge contributed important aspects to the new religion. Mohammed adopted the strict monotheism of the Old Testament, and "There is no God but Allah, and Mohammed is his Prophet" became the creed of Islam. Mohammed did not consider Jesus the Messiah, but one of a succession of prophets, and he rejected the doctrine of the Trinity.

Initially Mohammed was sure that he would succeed in converting many Christians and particularly the Jews to the belief that he was God's latest emissary. There were indeed many points of contact with Judaism. The Arabs considered themselves to be descendants of Abraham through his son Ishmael, practiced circumcision, and were forbidden to eat the meat of the pig. Yet Mohammed was to be disappointed. The Jews did not acknowledge him, and he expressed his anger in the Koran, the Holy Scripture of Islam which he largely inspired.

Among the Arab tribes his doctrine was even more quickly accepted. The new faith released in them vast, predominantly aggressive forces, and in less than one hundred years Islam conquered Persia, Syria, and Egypt. In the course of these conquests, the Jewish communities too were frequently drawn into bloody battles. Jerusalem was conquered by Omar, one of the first caliphs.

Where the old Temple had stood, a mosque was now erected, which was called the "dome on the rock." Mohammed had originally intended to make Jerusalem the Holy City of the Moslems (or "true believers"), but eventually he chose Mecca, partly because of his disappointment in the Jews.

In the conquered regions the Jews and the Christians were generally subject to certain restrictions; for example, they were not permitted to ride horses or to carry arms. Above all, they were taxed heavily, though in return they were assured of protection by the Moslem authorities.

Internal Jewish developments coinciding with the birth of the new religion resulted in new spiritual stirrings among the Jews of the Middle East. At least one sect was formed which rejected the Talmud and retained only the Bible. The rabbis were forced to reorient their thinking and to take a position with regard to the sects as well as to the philosophy and science of their time. The most famous Jewish places of learning in the Middle East were situated near Baghdad, which since A.D. 749 had been the residence of the caliphs. These academies of learning were situated in the cities of Sura and Pumbedita. At the academy of Pumbedita semi-annual conferences were held to which came all the eminent Talmud scholars of the land. They often lasted for a month and were attended by as many as four hundred students.

The Situation in Spain

It was, however, in Moslem Spain that Jewish theology, poetry, and science reached their greatest flowering. The Arabs had invaded Spain in A.D. 711, and would have reached France had they not been stopped by Charles Martel in 732. In the northern part of the Spanish peninsula a number of small Christian states remained, while in the South the conquerors created their own caliphate with Cordoba as capital. When this caliphate disintegrated in the course of succession disputes, a number of independent principalities arose, such as Seville, Granada, and Malaga, each headed by an Emir. In Cordoba and Granada especially, the Jews stood in high favor with the Moslem rulers. They became ministers, were sought after as physicians, and respected as astronomers. Some of them became known throughout the Arab world. They preferred to speak and write in Arabic, and produced a number of outstanding works in that language. The encounter between Jewish and Arab culture was so fruitful that it broadened all intellectual horizons and also left its mark on Christianity. Among many names we have chosen two as an example: Bahya ben Joseph ibn Pakuda and Moses ben Maimon.

In the year A.D. 1080 Bahya ben Joseph ibn Pakuda of Saragossa wrote one of the most popular of Jewish books, *The Duties of the Heart*. Bahya emphasized the obligations of the heart. He wrote on how to deal with the joys and sorrows of life, exhorting his readers to have confidence in God and to examine their conscience, which would make them into vessels of divine strength. By giving up everything not essential to life, and by maintaining an inner silence, men could prepare themselves to be invaded by God's love. A combination moral and mystical guide, Bahya's work retained its influence far beyond its time.

Quite different in emphasis and of considerable import for the non-Christian world was the work of Moses ben Maimon, usually called Maimonides. His first work was a new commentary on the Mishna, which was to enable talmudic scholars to understand this part of the Talmud without having to labor over the often confusing and intricate interpretations of the Gemara. He then tackled the tremendous task of rearranging the contents of the entire Talmud and to refashion from this labyrinth a lucid, systematically constructed code. He wrote this work in exemplary Hebrew. It came to be of fundamental importance for the further development of Judaism, for it gave logical explanations for the chief principles of Jewish doctrine. Finally, at the age of fifty-five, Maimonides gathered the sum of his wisdom in a book called *Guide for the Perplexed*. This magnificent attempt to reconcile theology and philosophy greatly influenced Thomas Aquinas, the most outstanding Christian theologian of the Middle Ages.

While Bahya ibn Pakuda had praised moral perfection—the duties of the heart—as the highest good, Maimonides saw the supreme goal as being the knowledge of God and the world, that is, intellectual perfection. The great spiritual renaissance of Judaism during that period is mirrored in this abundance of fertile contrasts.

Maimonides had been born in Spain, but all his writing was done in Cairo, for the peaceful coexistence of Islam and Judaism in Spain had come to an abrupt end in the middle of the twelfth century. Fanatical Moslems from North Africa, the so-called Almohades, invaded Spain in order to conquer their fellow Moslems and force them to become more orthodox believers. Unwilling to tolerate those of a different faith, the Almohades destroyed the synagogues and forced the Jews to either convert or flee. The refugees turned to Africa, as did Maimonides, or, in greater numbers, northward, finding refuge under the Christian princes of Castile, Aragon, and Navarre. These princes realized that the expatriates would become loyal and useful allies against the aggressive Almohades. Once more the Jews were granted a period of rest, during which their literature and poetry flourished anew. Then here, too, during the period of the Crusades, the darkness set in again over Judaism.

6

Persecution and Loyalty to the Faith

The Crusades

Toward the end of the eleventh century a rumor spread through Europe that the Moslems were desecrating the Holy Places of Christianity in Palestine and that pious Christian pilgrims were being maltreated. As a consequence, Pope Urban II, at a Church Council in 1095, called upon princes and knights to save the Holy Sepulchre from the hands of the infidels. Participation in this noble enterprise was to bring remission of sins. The Pope could hardly have foreseen the gigantic movement his words were to unleash. Within a year huge armies had been mustered. Their members had sewn the cross on their cloaks as a symbol of their holy mission. Knights who hoped to gain military glory were joined by peasants intent on escaping serfdom and oppressive taxation. Men of piety were accompanied by adventurers and opportunists lured by the riches of the distant East. The lowest elements of the populace, thieves, arsonists, and whores, eager for loot, also followed the crusaders. For two hundred years these motley crowds, which were often without formal leadership while they wound their way through Europe, were a terror and mortal danger to the Jewish communities, particularly in France and Germany. A contemporary Jewish chronicler describes the "wild, unbridled, relentless mob" which gathered under the sign of the cross, and continues:

As they passed through towns with Jewish inhabitants they said to each other, "We have left our homes to wreak vengeance upon the Ishmaelites, but see these Jews, whose ancestors have crucified our Savior —let us revenge ourselves on them above all! May the name of Israel be destroyed if they do not become like us and acknowledge Jesus as the Messiah!"

The first Jewish communities to fall victim to this primitive thirst for revenge and plunder were those in Rouen and other French cities. The news of the terror soon crossed the Rhine and the Jews of Mainz sent an emissary to Emperor Henry IV, their protector. He immediately ordered all dukes and bishops to shield the Jews from violence, but he lacked the necessary means to ensure that his orders were carried out everywhere. Therefore, after the throngs of crusaders had crossed the Rhine they were able to attack the Jews of Speyer, Worms, Mainz, and Cologne without hindrance.

In Worms a number of Jews had sought refuge in the bishop's palace. After the mob had looted all the Jewish homes and murdered those Jews who had remained behind, it camped outside the palace and offered the Jews the choice between baptism and death, between church and execution. The Jews asked for time to consider. When the period was up and the room in which they had hidden was opened, it contained only corpses. The Jews had preferred to kill each other and themselves rather than abandon their faith and fall into the hands of their merciless enemies.

The Jews of Mainz were forewarned by these events and tried to offer resistance to the hordes of the Jew-hater Emicho. In the end they too took refuge in the courtyard of the bishop's palace, but in vain. A surviving Jewish chronicler recorded what happened next:

When the children of Israel realized that their fate was sealed . . . they encouraged each other: "Let us bear everything that our faith demands from us with confidence and fortitude. . . . Soon our enemies will kill us . . . but it matters not if only our souls enter into Eden's eternal day! Blessed is he who suffers death in the name of the Only One . . ." Then they all exclaimed in chorus: "There is not time to lose! The enemy is near! Let us sacrifice ourselves without delay to the honor of God!" . . . When the enemy entered the courtyard he found the following: Wrapped in their prayer shawls the pious men sat with our

Rabbi Isaac ben Moses in the middle of the yard. He was the first to offer his neck and his head soon rolled on the ground. The others, in the meantime, had readied themselves to fulfill the will of the Creator. The enemy hurled arrows and stones at them, but our people did not move. All were killed. Upon seeing this, those who were in the rooms within preferred to die by their own hand . . . fathers sacrificed their sons, brothers their sisters, mothers their daughters, neighbors their neighbors, bridegrooms their brides. Each one sacrificed and was sacrificed in turn. . . . Whoever has heard or seen such happenings?

In Cologne whole families threw themselves into the Rhine with the cry "Hear, O Israel! The LORD is our God, the LORD alone." The Jews of Trier were equally ready to die for their faith but were prevented from committing suicide and were forcibly baptized.

In Regensburg the Jews were driven into the Danube, a cross was laid on the surface of the water, and they were forced to immerse themselves. (Later, Emperor Henry IV permitted all those who had been subjected to baptism by this and similar means to return to their own faith.)

The cross had become a symbol of terror to the Jews. The brutality and cruelty of the attempts to subject them to the Savior whom God, according to Christian teaching, had sent out of love for mankind, and the naked hatred which met them in the eyes of his fanatic adherents, could only lead them to believe this Savior to be a harbinger of disaster. Although there were great and noble Christians, such as Bernard of Clairvaux, who tried to restrain the savagery of the fanatics, the ranks of the persecutors also included priests, among them Peter of Cluny and the monk Radulf, who preached that every Crusade must begin with the conversion or extermination of the Jews. Peter of Cluny wrote to the King of France:

Why need we seek the enemies of Christ in far-off countries while the blaspheming Jews, who are more evil than the Saracens, live in our midst and mock Christ and the sacred relics of the Church with impunity? I do not demand that these people, who are under the curse, be put to death, for we are enjoined not to kill. God does not want them to be destroyed, but like Cain, who murdered his brother, they are to continue to exist under great suffering and in great shame so that life may be more bitter for them than death. They are dependent, miserable, oppressed, and fearful, and must remain so until they have found the path to salvation.

If one reads these words and thinks of the gospel, which means "good tidings," one realizes with horror the darkness that had descended on Christendom at that time. Even the most venerable assemblies, such as the Fourth Lateran Council, which met in Rome in 1215, were affected by it. This council had to deal with the first heretics in the South of France; imputing a connection between heretics and Jews, it issued a number of proclamations against the latter. The Jews were, for example, ordered to wear special clothes which distinguished them from the rest of the population, the intention doubtless being to brand them with the "mark of Cain," of which Peter of Cluny had spoken. This took the form of either the "yellow patch," which had to be worn on the outer garment, or the pointed hat. In this the Christians imitated the Moslems, who had forced both Christians and Jews under their rule to wear such marks of shame.

Superstition and Delusion

The centuries that followed have rightly been called the "Dark Ages." It seemed that all the light had been extinguished that the apostles in the name of Jesus had proclaimed: "I am the light of the world." The brutal masses knew nothing of love and mercy. They were filled with superstitions and delusions; they were bloodthirsty and vicious. Life had little value. Punishment was unbelievably cruel: the torture rack had been introduced into legal process, and produced the desired "evidence" for the most absurd of accusations. Again and again the Jews were the hardest hit in those difficult times, as the superstitious masses saw in them Satan and his henchmen.

In the twelfth century we find for the first time the accusation of ritual murder leveled against the Jews. According to this outrageous lie, the Jews were accused of needing the blood of a Christian person for ritual purposes connected with the celebration of Passover. Any fatal incident that was not immediately accounted for could set off a massacre of the Jews. In Blois, France, thirty-eight

Jews were burned at the stake because a hostler maintained that cne evening he had seen a Jew throw the corpse of a child into the river. In Troyes the corpse of a Christian was first hidden in the house of the wealthy and learned Jew Isaac Chatelin; then the crowd was led there to discover the "crime." The house was looted and all its inhabitants handed over to the Inquisition. All those involved refused to convert to save their lives and died at the stake. A missive sent by Pope Innocent IV to the archbishops and bishops of Germany in 1247, is shocking evidence of the interplay of superstition and greed in these atrocities:

We have received urgent supplications from Jews, stating that many spiritual and secular dignitaries and other nobles and officials in your cities and dioceses are fabricating godless accusations against the Jews in order to plunder them and confiscate their property. These men seem to have forgotten that it is the ancient Scriptures of the Jews that bear witness to the message of Christ. While the Holy Scripture laid down the commandment "Thou shalt not kill," and enjoins the Jews not even to touch a dead person during Passover, the false accusation is leveled against the Jews that for this feast they eat the heart of a murdered child. Whenever the body of a person is found whose killer is not known, the Jews are accused of having perpetrated the murder. These are, however, only excuses to persecute them in a most cruel fashion. Without any of the safeguards of legal process and in contempt of the privileges that have been graciously granted them by the Apostolic See they are robbed of their possessions in a godless and unjust manner, subjected to imprisonment, starvation and other tortures and condemned to a shameful death. In this manner the Jews are suffering even more under such princes and rulers than did their ancestors under the Pharaohs of Egypt.

This missive urged the bishops to protect the Jews. The emperors, too, took a position against the accusations of ritual murder and gave leading rabbis the opportunity to refute them publicly. But these admonitions and attempts at enlightenment did not reach the half-pagan, superstition-ridden masses, whose rage was aroused the more easily the more absurd the tale.

After the Fourth Lateran Council had proclaimed as dogma that bread and wine are changed into the body and blood of Christ during the Mass, the sacramental wafer became a favorite object of magic—and immediately the Jews were suspected of piercing these wafers in order to kill Christ again. A completely innocuous and natural process, the accumulation of red microbes on the wafers, was used as evidence, and these supposedly "bleeding" wafers gave rise to untold persecutions.

The ignorant confusion of the masses reached its climax in 1348, when bubonic plague invaded Europe and took its dreadful toll. In the same way that the pagan world had once considered the Christians to be the source of every adversity, now the Christians in turn considered the small, defenseless group of Jews to be the originators of all misfortune. They were held responsible for the plague and accused of having poisoned the wells. The absurdity of this accusation must have been obvious to everyone as the Jews fell victim to the plague as much as their Christian neighbors. But in Savoy, where this accusation first appeared, a Jewish physician was tortured until he admitted everything that had been suggested to him: that he and a few co-religionists had brewed a poison out of dried snakes, frogs, and scorpions, the dough of sacred wafers, and the hearts of Christian people and that they had sent this poison to Jews in other towns with the purpose of polluting the wells. Although the Pope explicitly took issue with such nonsensical tales of horror, they were believed just the same. Records show that about three hundred Jewish communities were wiped out as a result of these accusations.

In these barbarous times it also happened that without any excuse or superstitious provocation, bands of marauders roved through the countryside killing Jews. In Alsace, for instance, they terrorized the Jewish population with the battle cry "Avenge the Crucified One!"

Hatred and Greed

Superstitions and delusions alone could not have caused the terrible excesses we have described, had they not been combined with greed and hatred. The Christian merchants, having formed guilds of their own, gradually excluded the Jews from mercantile enterprise. All that remained for them was the indispensable but also dangerous and hated business of money-lending. The church's prohibtion of charging interest had remained in force, and the Jews had become the creditors of Christian Europe. As those who joined the Crusades were promised not only remission of sins but also dispensation from payment of interest, notes of hand were often formally burned when Jews were massacred. Many an ecclesiastic or secular prince may, therefore, not have proceeded with sufficient severity against the perpetrators of these crimes because he himself was indebted to the Jews, and hoped to rid himself of his creditors.

At times the French and English kings too practiced a most shameless form of extortion. Philip Augustus of France one Sabbath day ordered the Jews who were assembled in all the synagogues to be arrested and relieved of their money and their holiday garb. They were let go only after they had deposited a large amount as ransom. A few months later he released all Christians from their financial obligations to Jews on condition that they pay a fifth of these debts into the royal treasury. Eventually, his insatiable greed prompted him to expel the Jews from his crown lands in order to seize everything they could not carry with them. His successor, Philip the Handsome, was even more brutal; he drove the Jews out of the country, allowing them to take only a minimum amount of money and the clothes on their backs. He then auctioned off all their possessions and relentlessly collected the money his Christian subjects had owed them.

The kings of England habitually imposed high penalties on the Jews under the pretext, for example, that a Jewish physician had treated a Christian unsuccessfully and had therefore "killed him." This regime of exploitation and persecution became so oppressive in England that the Jews requested the King to permit them to emigrate. He denied their plea and once again demanded vast tributes from them. It was Edward I who finally decided to drive the Jews out of England completely, having first imprisoned all the heads of families in order to extort a ransom of twelve thousand pounds. In 1290 the Jews left England and did not return for almost four hundred years.

In Germany, too, the Jews had to pay dearly for "protection," but here their exploitation was less wholesale because the Emperor left the mulcting of his "protégés" to the feudal lords and the municipal authorities.

Steadfastness and Loyalty to the Faith

Out of the night that had descended upon the minds and hearts of men, the religious loyalty and steadfastness of the Jews shines like a precious diamond, whose hardness and purity is not affected by being trodden underfoot. No shrines were erected to the many thousand martyrs of Judaism, as this would have been regarded as idolatry. But they were commemorated in mournful and moving chants, and their names were recited on special days of commemoration, which sadly grew in number during these bitter centuries. A dark cloud of melancholy descended on the Jews of the West, and even after the shadow of the cross had ceased being a threat, the mourning of centuries could still be seen in many Jewish eyes.

One of the greatest scholars, Pierre Abelard, wrote in the period between the first and second Crusades:

No nation has suffered as much for God as the Jews. Dispersed among the nations, without kings or secular princes, they are oppressed by heavy taxation as if every day they were to ransom their lives anew. To mistreat them is considered laudable in the eyes of God, for the Christians imagine that Jewish suffering must be caused by God's extreme hatred for them. The Jews are at the mercy of their most relentless enemies. Even in their sleep they are oppressed by dreams of terror. They have no refuge but in Heaven. If they wish to travel even to a nearby town they have to pay large sums to obtain the protection of the Christian prince, who in truth desires their death in order to confiscate their possessions. The Jews cannot own vineyards or arable land, as no one will guarantee their right of ownership. Thus, money lending is their only way of making a living, but this in turn earns them even greater hatred from the Christians.

Deprived of all rights, and living in a state of total insecurity, the Jews resorted to forming increasingly tightly knit groups in their neighborhoods and shutting themselves off more and more from the outside world. In the face of constant danger they huddled together like sheep in fear of the wolves. Here, within their own community, they were able to give vent to their bitterness. Every new act of persecution led to greater estrangement between Jews and Christians. Christ, in whose name the most vicious atrocities were committed, became a symbol of loathing and horror for the people of the Old Covenant.

The Suffering of the Marranos

In these circumstances it is understandable that those Jews who submitted to forced conversion could not embrace their new faith with sincere conviction or enthusiasm. If at all possible, they tried to revert to their former belief; in general, the Jews preferred martyrdom to baptism.

Mass conversions took place only in one country, Spain, in the fourteenth century, with wealthy and influential members of the community often taking the lead. The reason may have been that in Spain the Jews had lived peaceably with the Christians for centuries. Many more were ready to convert than to die for their faith. They may have hoped to be able to return to the faith of their fathers later, but this they were not permitted to do. Instead, they were closely supervised by the clergy, who made sure that they were following the church's rituals faithfully.

Suspiciously watched by their new co-religionists and treated with contempt by their former brethren, these "new Christians" were burdened by great conflicts of conscience. The populace called them contemptuously Marranos ("swine"). As most of them had embraced Christianity out of fear rather than conviction, they now tried to resolve their inner conflict by following Christian ritual outwardly, while remaining Jews and observing the Sabbath and the dietary laws secretly. Such a double life was naturally accompanied by much spiritual torment, and could not always be kept concealed.

The Catholic clergy soon became aware of the peculiar habits of the new Christians, and the Inquisition, which had been instituted to combat heresy, was used against the Marranos. In 1478 Pope Sixtus IV gave permission for a special national Inquisition to be established in the united kingdom of Aragon and Castile. It was headed by the notorious Tomas de Torquemada. The new tribunal published thirty-seven criteria for identifying heresy and enjoined all Christians to report any suspects. Among the criteria were wearing festive clothing on Saturday, giving preference to certain kinds of meat and wine, reading the Psalms without ending them with the phrase "Honor to the Father and the Son," and many other such telltale signs. All denunciations were accepted without investigation, and the jails were soon filled with Marranos. Torture was used to obtain the necessary admissions, and the victims were then burned alive, watched by the royal court and large crowds. These were the so-called *autos-da-fé* ("acts of faith"). The tribunal of the Inquisition traveled rapidly from city to city. At first the Marranos were invited to show contrition and voluntary reconciliation with the church. Those who responded had to do penance, walking through the streets in a sinner's garb, the *sanbenito,* and to donate half their property to the "Holy War" of the Inquisition. In addition, they had to demonstrate the sincerity of their repentance by denouncing other Marranos. Those who remained "irreconciled" were tortured again and again (new tortures were ordered after every disavowal) until they admitted the crimes they were accused of. The *autos-da-fé* followed each other in close succession, with the entire property of the victims going to the King, who profited considerably from every "act of faith."

For a time the persecution of the Marranos gave the Spanish Jews a breathing space. But then the inquisitors decided that the recalcitrant new Christians could only be made into good Catholics if they were deprived of all contacts with Judaism. In 1492 the Spanish royal couple, Ferdinand and Isabella, ordered the expulsion of the Jews from their realm. This decree affected hundreds of thousands of people long settled in the country, whose ancestors had been buried in its soil for many generations. Their distress was indescribable.

Some of those banished from Spain went to Portugal, from which they were later also expelled. Others sought new homes in North Africa, in Italy, and in Turkey. They retained the Spanish language for hundreds of years and were called *Sephardim,* which is Hebrew for "Spaniards." Those who settled in Germany and Poland, on the other hand, were called *Ashkenazim.* Each group developed its own synagogue ritual. Their members also came to differ in physical appearance: the Sephardic Jews are predominantly dark-skinned and Oriental-looking, while many of the Ashkenazim are light-skinned, blond, and blue-eyed.

After the expulsion of the Jews from Spain the Marranos were no better off. The Inquisition continued to rage until the seventeenth century. Finally, the Marranos saw no other way but to flee. They sought a haven in France and, particularly, in Holland. Once there, they returned to Judaism, Christianity having become abhorrent to them. It is understandable that the new communities formed by former Marranos were particularly strict in the observance of Jewish law. The conflict of conscience which they had suffered for so many generations now turned into exaggerated religious zeal.

As a result, one of the greatest sons of the Jewish people, Baruch (Benedict) de Spinoza of Amsterdam, was expelled from the Jewish community in 1656 on religious grounds. The curse of banishment was placed upon him and no Jew was permitted to speak with or write to him. Spinoza's philosophy was indeed opposed to both the Jewish and the Christian concepts of God; he saw God as the substance of all things but not as the Creator who calls out to man and who in turn is called upon by man. Spinoza refused to convert to Christianity; he lived in poverty and solitude, a virtuous man and a true sage to whom life and dogma were one.

7

Jewish Piety: The Fruit of Suffering

"The Prepared Table"

During the centuries of oppression the Jews again and again derived renewed strength from their Holy Scriptures. The continued failure of all their earthly endeavors was but a repetition of the deep suffering the prophets had experienced. Job had borne undeserved and inexplicable misery, yet had not doubted God. The author of the Psalms had called out to God from the depths of despair, yet above the darkness which covered the earth the promise could always be heard: "For Thy light will come . . ."

The Jews were able to find comfort in their Scriptures and in the treasures of the Talmud. Maimonides wrote: "Our sufferings will not crush us; though our oppressors have been many, they have all perished; Israel's name will endure forever. Our sufferings are a touchstone, and it is our pride and glory to withstand them."

In addition to the often somewhat incomprehensible Talmud, more popular writings now became available. They spoke to the heart of the suffering people and provided guidelines for their daily life. One of these books was *Sefer Ha-Hasidim* ("The Book of the Pious"), a collection of sayings that made its appearance during the times of the Crusades. It enjoined the Jews to observe meticulously their duties toward those of different faiths so that none of their hostile neighbors would have cause to say "The Jews are dishonest." The book was a curious mixture of transcendental wisdom and a belief in magic and ghosts. One of its unforgettable stories is that of "The Shepherd Who Could Not Pray":

And he said every day: "Lord of the Universe, Thou knowest well that if Thou hadst a flock and gave it to me to watch I would do it for Thee without being paid—though everyone else pays me, for I love Thee." A wise man, who heard the shepherd pray, corrected him and taught him the prescribed prayers. The shepherd forgot what he was taught and prayed no more, since he did not dare to repeat his former words. But a voice spoke to the wise man in a dream and told him that he had done great wrong and that he was to go to the shepherd without delay so that he might pray again as he was wont. This he did, and the shepherd prayed again. This shows us that neither the Torah nor good works were needed here, only what one man felt to be good, and he was rewarded for it as if he had done a great deed, for the Merciful One desires the heart.

About three hundred years later Joseph Caro (1488–1575), who had been exiled from Spain as a child with his parents and had grown up in Turkey, wrote a digest of all the talmudic laws. He followed up this extensive scholarly work with a more popular summary, titling it aptly *Shulhan Arukh,* which means "The Prepared Table." This title was to convey the idea that every man could find nourishment at this table if he would but partake. The book became renowned throughout the diaspora. Its spirit can best be portrayed in Joseph Caro's own words: "Let all thy deeds be done in the name of Heaven so that those things that are freely given, such as eating, drinking, walking, sitting, standing, talking and all the necessities of your life . . . are done or satisfied in the service of the Creator, or become a means of serving Him." The earnestness with which the demand was made that every aspect of daily life be hallowed was bound to give a distinct cast to the Jewish character. The Jews, for the sake of the Covenant God had made with Israel, were to obey his Law faithfully. To be God's Chosen People was always both a crown of adornment and a yoke harnessing their striving.

The Secrets of the Kabbalah

The martyred people sought strength not only in moral maxims but also in passionate turning toward the transcendent in an attempt to penetrate the secrets of the supernatural world, thereby hastening the coming of redemption. This was the origin of the *Kabbalah* ("that which is received or handed down"), a system of Jewish mystic and secret lore. In the thirteenth century its teachings spread through France and Spain, at first only by word of mouth.

Soon they were gathered also in a book, which was called by one of its opening words, *Zohar,* which means "radiance." Its contents were attributed to one of the most famous rabbis of the second century A.D., Simon ben Yohai, but they were in fact a compendium of the writings of several anonymous Kabbalists. These men regarded the Bible as the supreme authority, but they were not satisfied with its manifest content. They read divine revelations into every sentence, word, and letter.

"Woe to the man," they wrote, "who imagines that the Torah contains the everyday histories and conversations of simpletons. Is it conceivable that the Almighty had no holy words for His Torah and had to depend on the insipid stories of Hagar and Esau, of Laban and Jacob, of Bileam and his ass in order to construct from them the Torah, which is called the Doctrine of Truth? . . . But the enlightened do not consider the outer garment but the body which it covers, some even look into the soul, i.e., the meaning of the Torah, so that in the next world they may behold God, the soul of souls. . . ."

A whole edifice of mysterious speculations was erected over the ancient text of the Scriptures. Ten spheres or intermediary forces were supposed to exist between God and the world of sinful men. By fervent prayer man could influence them directly. Each of these spheres had been given a number, and this was the origin of the Kabbalistic use of mystic numbers, which flourished all the more richly, since in Hebrew, numbers are expressed by letters.

When the Jews were driven from Spain, Kabbalistic mysticism received new stimulus. Many exiles settled in northern Galilee, in Safed, not far from the grave of Simon ben Yohai. In less than one hundred years Safed became a center of religious awakening and of

Kabbalism, with twenty-one synagogues and eighteen academies of talmudic learning. The so-called *Practical Kabbalah* originated in Safed.

Philosophical speculations were replaced by a pessimistic mysticism, in which the concept of the migration of souls played a major role. In keeping with the thinking of the times, the *Practical Kabbalah* was dominated by the belief in demons and miracles. It prepared the way for later generations of miracle workers and exorcisers. The German legend of Doctor Faustus may be deeply rooted in these concepts.

The Talmud Academies of Poland

The trend toward mysticism proved no obstacle to continued study and cultivation of the Talmud. The more the Christians attacked it, the more the Jews treasured this precious collection of venerable traditions. In 1242 a formal "trial" of the Talmud had taken place in Paris, based on the assertion that the Talmud contained defamations of Jesus. The trial ended in a Paris square with the burning of twenty-four wagonloads of volumes of the Talmud, collected from every corner of the land.

In Poland especially, the study of the Talmud flourished anew. In the face of persecution in Germany and France many Jews had fled eastward and had obtained the protection and support of the kings of Poland. They were not subjected to any occupational restrictions, and in a country that had until then only known peasants and nobles, Jews formed a middle class of merchants, artisans, physicians, administrators, and innkeepers.

They continued to use German as their everyday language, gradually enriching it with Hebrew words. Thus Yiddish was born, a language based on Middle High German and written in Hebrew characters. The immigrants set much store by the study of the Torah and learning in general. As the Polish state allowed them complete autonomy, they could arrange these matters as they saw fit. All boys aged six to thirteen were obliged to attend school, where they were taught arithmetic, reading, and writing, and particularly the study of the Bible and the easier parts of the Talmud. In addition there existed numerous academies for the study of the

Talmud, which were called *yeshivahs*. They were headed by a rabbi, who enforced strict discipline. He received a salary from the community to enable him to devote himself entirely to teaching and study. The students, too, received stipends. They were obligated to introduce younger boys to the study of the Talmud. The frequent seminars held in the House of Study were described by a contemporary chronicler as follows:

Anyone can present a difficult Talmudic question to the head of the Yeshivah, and he is always ready to analyze it in detail. He then calls an academic conference where he presents his own interpretation. Then a number of contradictory quotations from the Talmud or the commentaries are posited, their conflicts resolved by other quotations, conflicts again discovered in the latter, and they in turn resolved by quoting yet further passages. This process continues until the original question is finally clarified.

This method of intellectual fencing undoubtedly aided in the development of an uncommonly keen intellect, but sometimes deteriorated into an empty play of words. It was sharply criticized as a "useless waste of time, a lie and a deception" even by some of the rabbis themselves. But despite the occasional excesses of these seminars one would be wrong to overlook the fact that here a whole people held scholarship rather than riches in the highest esteem and invested it with supreme authority. These traditions remained alive in Poland until the twentieth century. We quote an experience described by Alfred Jeremias, a German theologian:

In Warsaw I once found a cab-stand full of cabs but without a single driver. At home I would have known where to find them, but here a Jewish boy showed me the way. At the other end of the yard, up one flight of stairs, were the rooms where the Jewish cabbies assembled. This was a Jewish house of adult study. There were two rooms, one filled with book shelves full of volumes of the Talmud, the other a meeting room for religious services. All the cabbies were eagerly studying or engaging in religious discussion. Later on I found out that the bakers, the butchers, the cobblers and every other trade has its own house of study and worship in the Jewish quarter and that every break in the workday is devoted to the study of the Torah. And when they meet one will often say to the other: "Let us discuss a bit of the Torah."

In the seventeenth century the most dreadful catastrophe befell this oasis of East European Judaism. It was overrun by murderous Ukrainian cossacks, who rose in rebellion against their Polish overlords. In 1648, under the leadership of Chmielnicki, they ravaged the land with fire and sword. Their hatred of the Jews was boundless and they rarely attempted to persuade the unfortunate to convert. These persecutions were characterized by hitherto-unknown atrocities. Children were torn apart or thrown into the fire before the eyes of their mothers, women were buried alive, men were skinned and mutilated. People must have thought that hell had let loose all the tormenting monsters that medieval painters had portrayed dragging the condemned to eternal punishment. The roads were choked with thousands of refugees trying to escape the murderous hordes. The famous rabbis of the Talmud schools died by the hundreds as martyrs for their faith. The total number of the dead was estimated at about one hundred thousand. From that time on, Polish Jews began to return to the West in the hope of finding a haven.

Hopes for the Coming of the Messiah

The devoted study of the supernatural secrets of the *Kabbalah* was in part connected with a reawakening of messianic hopes. By transposing the letters of Scripture into numbers according to mystical calculations, the Jews hoped to be able to discover when the Messiah would come. In view of the excess of their suffering it was natural that people asked again and again: "Has the time not come, is the cup of our bitterness not full, will Israel's Savior not appear to us now?"

Among the Jews in the Middle East fervent visionaries who considered themselves to be the Messiah had appeared several times and died a martyr's death. Now, after the terrible events in Poland which flooded all Europe with pitiable refugees, while at the same time the Inquisition was again burning Jews at the stake in Spain, Jewry was stirred to its depths. A great messianic movement began in the Middle East and quickly spread to the West. It centered around Sabbatai Zevi, whose great knowledge of the *Kabbalah* and the ascetic way of life deeply impressed his contemporaries. Perhaps because he was so greatly revered, he conceived the idea that he was the one for whom Israel was waiting, and in 1665 he proclaimed himself the Messiah. He sent missives to all the congregations outside of the Holy Land, setting off a wave of penitence and asceticism as well as joy and hope which few could resist. Merchants in Hamburg and Amsterdam got ready to embark for the Holy Land, which the self-proclaimed Messiah, Sabbatai Zevi, was about to win back for the Jews. In the meantime, however, he was taken prisoner when, without apparent purpose, he embarked on a journey to Constantinople. His followers regarded his arrest as but the inevitable last suffering before redemption; great numbers of them congregated around the jail where he was held and sent him gifts. The Sultan of Turkey finally decided to put an end to the matter. He gave Sabbatai Zevi the choice of embracing Islam or being put to death. Sabbatai preferred to live. Upon conversion he was permitted to leave the palace as Mehemed Effendi. His adherents did not at once become discouraged, but interpreted his defection as the nadir of degradation through which the Messiah had to pass. But in the end, they had to realize that they had been deluded. Eventually, occurences like these led to a purification of the messianic concept. It became evident that no one could declare himself to be the Messiah, that only God could reveal him.

Hasidism

In a most remarkable way we find that in the midst of darkest suffering and despair a new piety flowered in southern Poland which embraced the broad masses of the Jewish people. In contrast to talmudism, which enlightened the intellect, it appealed to the heart. The movement originated with a man who was born in the year 1700 in extreme poverty, worked variously as assistant to a schoolteacher, as custodian of a synagogue, as a ritual slaughterer, and as a cantor. He read the Kabbalistic texts and devoted himself with fervor to prayer and meditation. At the age of thirty-six he began to travel through the country and, with the aid of prayer, but also with amulets and medicinal herbs, to heal the sick and give advice for the future. His influence went beyond that of the ordinary miracle workers: the people saw in him a physician of the soul and gave him the name *Baal-Shem-Tov,* the "Master of the Good Name." After a few years he settled permanently in Miedziboz and gathered a group of disciples around him. In contrast to the false Messiahs he did not claim to be unique, but rather instructed his disciples to return to their hometowns, live there as *zaddikim* ("just men") and devote themselves to good works and to the building of a community of pious men (*Hasidim*). The spirit that emanated from these simple men, who walked with God in their everyday life, was so unusual that an inexhaustible fund of legends and stories grew up around them.

The foremost aim of the Hasidim was not as much the elucidation of Jewish doctrine as the rejuvenation of living. They set an example of how one can live both with God and in the world. One serves God, they said, by serving his creatures. God wants to use men for his works, and these works do not require special circumstances, but are part of everyday life. The spark of the Eternal is hidden in the most common and humdrum of everyday things and man can discover it by exercising loving care. For this reason the preacher Solomon said, "Whatever you do, do it with all your might." The most important moment is always the present; the most important human being is the one sitting next to you. In answer to the question, What was the most important thing for the Baal-Shem-Tov? one of his disciples said, "Whatever he was engaged in at the moment." In answer to the question, What is the first requirement in the service of God? the Baal-Shem answered, "For spiritual man: to love without mortification; for others: to learn to see that there is a holy light in everything corporeal and that everyone can be led back to this, their root, and be hallowed." For the Hasidim the love of man was the road to the love of God. A zaddik enlightened a disciple who did not know whether the love of God or the love of man took precedence: "We read in the prayer book that before a prayer we are to say, 'Love thy neighbor as thyself.' The true love of God begins with the love of man, and if someone says to you that he loves God but does not love men, you can be sure that he lies." The Baal-Shem-Tov himself explained the commandment of loving one's neighbor as follows: "You are to love your fellow man as you love yourself. And who knows better than you your many shortcomings? As you can love yourself despite them, so shall you love your neighbor—however many defects you may see in him."

Rabbi Pinchas of Koretz taught: "If a man despise you and injure you, you must be strong and love him more than before. Through such love you will help him to change. Therefore we are to love also the evil-doers, but we must hate their evil deeds." One of Pinchas' disciples is reported as having said that in intercourse with one's fellowmen love should not be measured, for an abundance of love must be given to make up for its lack in the world.

Hasidism flourished in Poland for generations. Jews were moved by their devotion to God to embrace both God and the world. In the end Hasidism's strength was weakened by the western Enlightenment.

8

Life in the Ghetto

Since the Babylonian exile the Jews in the diaspora had been accustomed to living near each other in order to preserve their faith and their laws. They lived within walking distance of their synagogues, as driving or riding was not permitted on the Sabbath and no religious service could be held unless ten men were present. Jewish neighborhoods were not particularly conspicuous, for in the Middle Ages it was the general custom to assign the various streets to different groups among the town's population; the weavers, the tanners, the bakers, the butchers, and the carpenters, as well as the Jews, each had their own streets.

Not until the fifteenth and sixteenth centuries did these voluntary or occasionally even privileged residential settlements of the Jews become the narrow and oppressive living quarters which have gained such wretched fame as "ghettos." The derivation of this name is not entirely clear. It probably originated in Venice, where the Council of the Republic decreed in 1516 that the Jews were to live in a special section of the city which, until then, had been called *ghetto nuovo,* or "new foundry." In the course of time this name may have been applied to all similar quarters. In 1566 when Paul IV became Pope he decreed the enclosing of the Jewish quarter in Rome. He also renewed all the former humiliating ordinances by which Jews were to be identified. In addition the Jews of Rome were forced to listen for many hours each week to a Christian sermon, which was supposed to convert them, while bailiffs watched that no one put wax in his ears or fell asleep.

The custom of surrounding the Jewish quarters with walls and gates that could be locked quickly spread through Europe. Jewish protests were usually in vain. Instead of being able to live together voluntarily, they were now isolated, as if suffering from leprosy or the plague. The ghetto usually consisted of one long street, and the gates at each end were locked every evening. Needless to say the wages of the gatekeepers had to be paid by the Jews. Most of the ghettos were already crowded when additional Jewish families who had lived elsewhere were forced to move into them. Through the natural increase in the population the situation became worse every year. The Christian authorities never thought of enlarging the ghetto, but preferred to order restrictions on Jewish marriages. At one time only twelve marriage licenses were issued each year in Frankfurt on Main for about 450 families.

The Frankfurt Ghetto

The Frankfurt ghetto may serve as an example of what life was like in a ghetto. Affixed to its gate was an ignominious painting depicting a child who had supposedly been murdered by Jews for ritual purposes as well as a Jew who was being trampled by a pig. The street itself was dark and so narrow that a carriage could not turn in it. Because of the lack of space the houses had been built very high so that their upper stories almost touched each other and very little light reached the street. There were about 190 houses, each inhabited by two or three families, that is, by thirteen to twenty people. The houses were marked by shields, from which they and their inhabitants later took their surnames, for example, "The Bear," "The Black Shield," "The Red Shield" (Rothschild).

The center of the community was the synagogue, also referred to as the "school." It served both as a place for religious services and as a hall for teaching and meetings. Three time a day Jewish men gathered in prayer, and here they also studied the Torah and the Talmud. In addition one could meet travelers from abroad at the synagogue and listen to their reports. Important legal decisions were also made here and justice administered. Next to the synagogue was a hostelry for transients, a hall where weddings and other festivities took place, and a bath house. There was also a ritual bath below ground, for which untouched underground water was used. Within the ghetto walls there was also a cemetery. According to Jewish custom the dead have an eternal right to their graves and cemeteries can, therefore, not be dug up or leveled. But at the same time the cemetery, as a symbol of the fleeting nature of life, is not decked with flowers like the Christian graveyards.

In 1709 the Frankfurt ghetto was inhabited by 225 merchants and storekeepers, 50 money changers and money lenders, 25 artisans and laborers, 35 members of the clergy and professional men, and 40 persons either without specified trade or in receipt of community relief. These figures clearly indicate that the Jews' exclusion from guilds and from owning landed property considerably limited their choice of occupation. Among the merchants the second-hand dealers played a leading role. Money was usually lent against security which, if not redeemed, was forfeited after a certain period. As a result many valuable items could be bought in the ghetto—jewelry, weapons, expensive apparel—which attracted many Christian buyers. The majority of the artisans were bakers and butchers, but there were also tailors, dyers, goldsmiths, and printers. The latter were indispensable because of the great demand for Hebrew books.

Among the clergy were the rabbis, some of whom had been invited from distant communities, Hebrew teachers, and ritual slaughterers. The position of the usher of the synagogue—called *shammes*—often became one of great importance, since he also served as a bailiff and carried out the sentences passed by the Jewish court of justice. The secular administration of the community was completely democratic in form. A council, consisting of seven persons, was elected by secret ballot, as were a magistrate and a treasurer, who often also served as dispenser of charities.

In one very important regard the Jewish administration was handicapped and able to function only as an executive arm of its Christian overlord. The emperors, princes, and city councils did not exact taxes from individual Jews but from the Jewish community as a whole. A glance at an ordinance issued by the Archbishop of Mainz in 1724 shows how exorbitant were the demands made on the Jews:

Money for the New Year, money on St. Martin's Day, payments due to the Cathedral Chapter from the synagogues, monies for the poor house, monies for the bells of St. Emmeran, alehouse imposts due to the receiver of rents, monies for the poor students of the Jesuits, money for fish for the Franciscans, Capuchins and Jesuits, Palatinate passage money, money for the rural constable . . .

The Jewish council was responsible for the collection of these (usually large) sums. In these circumstances it was not possible to tax all inhabitants of the ghetto equitably. The wealthy had to bear the main burden whether they wanted to or not and thus became the most influential members of the council. This resulted in social tensions which, fortunately, never grew so severe as to endanger Jewish solidarity in times of stress.

The Consequences of the Ghetto System

In the Middle Ages it was in many ways to the advantage of the Jews to live as they did in a closed community. Leo Baeck, one of the outstanding rabbis of our century, has rightly said that the three great evils from which Europe suffered in the Middle Ages— brutality, drunkenness, and ignorance—could not enter the gates of the ghetto. But the closer we move to modern times, the more the world surrounding the ghetto changed, the more the existence of the ghetto itself had to be considered a wretched remnant of past barbarity.

The enforced isolation and miserable living conditions contributed to a deepening of the gulf between Jews and Christians. In Goethe's *Dichtung und Wahrheit* we find a vivid picture of how strange the ghetto appeared, even to an unprejudiced mind:

Among the experiences that oppressed the boy as well as the adolescent were, in particular, the conditions of the Jewish quarter or the Jews' Alley, as it was called, which in former times must have been caged in between the walls of the city and the moat. The narrowness, the dirt, the milling crowds, the unappealing accents of the language, all combined to create a most unattractive impression, even if one only happened to cast a glance through the gates. It was a long time before I dared to enter it by myself.

The Jews themselves, of course, suffered the most from these conditions. The unhealthy overcrowding in the ghetto, the dark streets, the almost exclusive pursuit of urban occupations, the severance of connections with the countryside, and the frequent marriages between relatives inevitably affected the physical and mental constitution of the ghetto inhabitants. The effects were similar to those we can observe today in people forced to grow up in the big city slums.

The Jews, however, suffered not only from the handicaps under which they had to live, but also from the hatred of the surrounding population and the resulting insecurity and danger. The ghetto was by no means a place where people lived in stultifying isolation, but rather one which heightened the anxieties and sensibilities of its inhabitants. The Jewish merchants, who traveled far and wide, carried news from place to place, and all the world events were eagerly followed inside the ghetto. Having for centuries served as the scapegoats for every disaster, the Jews asked themselves at every turn of events: Will this be to our benefit, or will it hurt us? In such circumstances the inhabitants of the ghetto could hardly achieve mental equanimity. They lived under constant tension.

As soon as they left the ghetto, they encountered numerous humiliations. They were forced to wear yellow patches or yellow hats, to pay an infamous head tax at turnpikes, and often to step into the gutter to make room for Christians. They had to bear being the object of much ill-considered "fun," even from children.

They found some solace for these degradations in the warmth of their family life, the dignified observance of their religious laws, and the joyful celebration of their festivals, without which Judaism is inconceivable.

When the sabbath candles were lit, the people in the ghetto threw off all the drudgery of everyday life. All humiliations were cast off. The love of the Creator, which every seventh day was given back to the Jews, also brought with it a return of their honor and their dignity as human beings in their lowly abodes. . . . On the sabbath and on the feast days joy reigned in the ghetto, however much misery may have embittered the week. To feel joy at the festivals was a religious obligation which became a vital necessity in Jewish consciousness.

—Hermann Cohen

But the contrasts were too great, and often they led to the oscillating mood and nervous demeanor that were frequently characteristic of the ghetto Jews. Together with the spirituality produced by the one-sided study of the Talmud, this psychological condition was often misread as an innate feature of the Jewish character. In fact, however, this behavior was only a reaction to a hostile and dangerous environment. These characteristics were as little inherited as the language that developed under the influence of Hebrew in the isolation of the ghetto. This became quite obvious when the gates of the ghetto were thrust open.

9

The End of Segregation

Humanism and the Reformation

In the fifteenth century ancient Greek philosophy and art were rediscovered in Italy. This renaissance also brought with it a new kind of critical thinking, a new understanding of the laws of nature and of scientific research. In the Middle Ages the church had determined and limited people's thinking, but now man, more conscious of his gifts, refused to be confined any longer. Scholars, for whom man came to be the measure of all things, focused interest on man's nature, dignity, capacity, and insight.

One of the most eminent scholars in Germany was Johannes Reuchlin. He had not only studied the writings of the Greeks, but had been especially interested in Hebrew, the original language of the Old Testament. In 1509, because of his knowledge of Hebrew, he became involved in a rather dangerous affair. A baptized Jew by the name of Pfefferkorn, who—like so many apostates—joined in the persecution of his former co-religionists with particular fervor, asked Reuchlin to lend his expert talents to an indictment of the talmudic writings. Reuchlin refused and Pfefferkorn submitted his indictment to the Emperor without Reuchlin's assistance. When Reuchlin was later invited to give his opinion, he conscientiously advised against the destruction of Jewish books. However, the matter was not allowed to rest there because the Dominican monks, as the official inquisitors, were determined to achieve a condemnation of the Talmud. All the important German humanists, among them Erasmus of Rotterdam and Philip Melanchthon, took Reuchlin's side. Ulrich von Hutten, as courageous with his pen as with his sword, also joined the fray, satirizing the obtuse and superstitious thinking of the monks in his famous "Obscurantist Letters" (*Epistolae Obscurorum Virorum*).

Martin Luther, too, took Reuchlin's part, although he had no liking for the Talmud and shared the opinion held by many within the church that the Jews had been condemned by God. But he hoped that the pure gospel preached by him and based solely on the text of the New Testament would deliver the Jews from their impenitence and save at least some of them from the wrath of God. He felt that if the Jews were to be won over, it would be foolish to make them abhor Christianity by treating them with hatred and violence. This was the tenor of a missionary tract which he wrote a few years after he had published his ninety-five theses in Wittenberg. It points out "that Jesus was a Jew," and states further, "The Jews have been treated like dogs, they have been insulted and robbed of their belongings . . . and yet they are kinsmen, cousins and brothers of our Saviour. No other people have been singled out as they have to be entrusted by God with the Holy Scriptures."

This invitation to extend the hand of friendship to the Jews, to consort with them, and to admit them to all occupations and employment was revoked by Luther twenty years later in violent and even brutal language. He was perhaps disappointed that the reformation of Christianity had tempted so few Jews to convert. But even more important was the fact that the study of the Bible, which the Reformation had made possible among large groups of people, led to a new appreciation of the Jews' devout adherence to their laws. Among the Baptist sects a handful of people had converted to Judaism. Luther became so concerned over this development that, like the popes of the time of the Lateran Council, he demanded that the Jews be subjected to the most stringent segregation. In his pamphlet "Of the Jews and their Lies" he advised the Christian authorities to burn the synagogues, demolish the Jews' homes, destroy the Talmud, prohibit the rabbis from teaching, suspend their right of free travel, and forbid them to engage in finance, allowing them instead to work only in the meanest of occupations. As a last resort he recommended that they be expelled altogether.

As author of this shameful and hate-filled pamphlet the aging and gloomy reformer thus became responsible for instilling an ancient poison into the life of the new Christian movement. Hence Protestantism, as well as Roman Catholicism, has been a source of anti-Semitic feelings down to our time.

Nevertheless, the Reformation, coupled with humanism, eventually led to the coexistence of all the various sects and religions. As a first step, the principle that every sovereign should decide the religion of his subjects was agreed upon. The different Christian denominations thus existed side by side, but without really tolerating each other. The Thirty Years' War (1618–48) demonstrated how enormous the tensions were between them.

The first example of true religious tolerance appeared in North America, in Providence, Rhode Island. Roger Williams, the city's founder, wrote:

God does not demand that in a civil state a uniform religion be established and enforced, for such enforced uniformity will sooner or later offer the greatest opportunity for civil strife, for the oppression of conscience, the persecution of Christ and his servants, hypocrisy and the destruction of millions of souls.

Faithful to these principles, Providence not only allowed Christians of all denominations to settle within the city and enjoy equal rights, but also offered a refuge to Jews, permitting them to practice their religion freely and admitting them to all civic offices.

The Enlightenment

While in the New World these reforms could be realized speedily, in the Old World it remained for thinkers and poets to prepare the intellectual foundation for change. Humanism led to the Enlightenment. The great concept was born that all men, be they Frenchmen or Germans, nobles, burghers, or peasants, black or white, Christians or non-Christians, are united by their humanity, that God has granted them the light of reason and the ability to recognize the good and act on it. Man's innate capacities and his dignity were now held in high regard. The word *humanity* came to mean brotherliness, mutual aid, respect for everything human, and the renunciation of revenge and brute force. These sentiments gave birth to the tremendous changes which led to our present legal and political forms of government. Torture was abolished as a senseless and cruel procedure that produces, not the truth, but lies; slavery and serfdom were condemned and equality before the law was demanded for all citizens. Freedom of conscience was to be granted to everyone in matters of faith because religious truths could not be demonstrated by reason, and to force them upon others contradicted their very essence.

This new outlook penetrated the darkest corners of superstition and put an end to the belief in witches, one of the then-current throwbacks to paganism. It was also of the greatest importance to the Jews. Their faith was now—like Islam—granted official sanction. They were no longer regarded as obdurately refusing to recognize the truth of Christian dogma. This inevitably brought about the demand that they also be treated as human beings with equal rights, liberated from the degradation of the ghetto, and put on an equal footing with Christian citizens.

Gotthold Ephraim Lessing and Moses Mendelssohn

These sentiments were set forth most impressively by the German poet Gotthold Ephraim Lessing in his drama *Nathan the Wise*. He had fashioned the main character, Nathan, a noble and wise Jew, after Moses Mendelssohn. The latter had grown up in Dessau as the son of a poor Torah scribe, and while still a boy had devoted himself to the study of the Talmud and Maimonides with such fervor that he had acquired a permanent curvature of the spine. But, as he often joked later, although his spine had been bent, his spirit had been uplifted. When he went to live in Berlin at the age of fourteen, he learned Latin and German so quickly that he was soon familiar with the whole field of the philosophy of his time. He earned his livelihood there first as a tutor and then as a bookkeeper and business manager of a Jewish silk manufacturer.

He became acquainted with Lessing through a letter occasioned by Lessing's drama *The Jews*. In this play, too, Lessing had created the character of a noble and unselfish Jew instead of the usual caricature of the Jewish usurer. A Goettingen professor maintained in a criticism of the play that so honorable a Jew could hardly be true to life. On reading this, Mendelssohn felt "most ashamed" as he wrote to a friend:

What a degradation for our oppressed people! What exaggerated contempt. . . . In truth, how can any man with even a trace of integrity, deny that an entire nation is capable of producing a single honest man? . . . Let them continue to oppress us, to force us to live in isolation among the free and happy citizens, let them even continue to expose us to the mockery and contempt of the world, but let them not deprive us completely of the reputation of virtue, the only solace of the oppressed and the only refuge of the abandoned. . . .

The recipient of this letter passed it on to Lessing and thus initiated the friendship between the two men. Lessing encouraged Mendelssohn to write for publication and erected a permanent literary monument to his friend in the character of "Nathan." In this play the relationship between Judaism, Christianity, and Islam is illustrated by an old fable about a man who possessed a ring with a magic stone, which he could leave to only one of his three sons. In order not to hurt any of them he had copies made of it and gave one ring to each son. Thus each of them thought he had inherited the magic ring. After their father's death they discovered the well-meant deception and asked the judge which of the three rings was the magic one. The judge gave them this advice: "If each of you has his ring from his father, let each one believe that his is the genuine one. Well then! Let each of you emulate your father's genuine, unprejudiced love and each compete with his brother in demonstrating the power of the stone in his ring. Let each augment his fervor with gentleness and loving kindness, with charity and devotion to God!"

The play's message was that in the future the truth of the different religions was to be tested, not by dogmatic conflict, but by the exercise of love and by a piety that would permeate every phase of life.

The Court Jews

Although the feeling engendered by the Enlightenment was a powerful force in those days, it alone could not have led the Jews out of the ghetto. Combined with changes in economic life, however, it went a long way. After the Thirty Years' War the German empire had been divided and subdivided into small and sometimes minute territories, ruled by kings, dukes, and princes, who as absolute rulers of their subjects endeavored to bring about the economic recovery of their principalities. They fostered trade and industry and promoted particularly the establishment of factories, in which a division of labor could be carried out that made production cheaper and quicker than in the old-fashioned workshops. Such profitable undertakings could not be started without capital. For this, one had to turn to the Jews, who, as pointed out previously, had been forced into the occupation of money-lending during the Middle Ages.

The princes' need for capital led to the extension of privileges to a select few Jews. Individual Jewish families received special letters of protection which granted them some rights notwithstanding the remaining restrictions. They could live outside the ghetto and, in part, could pass this right on to their descendants. The minting of money was particularly often entrusted to these families. For example, Frederick the Great of Prussia leased the right to coin money to the Ephraim family, who were Berlin money dealers. In order to fill the royal coffers he ordered them to mint debased money. Such manipulations diverted the people's anger over the devaluation of the currency from the King to the "mint Jews," and thus lowered the reputation of the Jews even further.

The Jews were used for similar diversionary maneuvers at the courts of the smaller principalities. They were appointed "Court Jews" and put in charge of the management of the country's finances. The financial adviser of the Duke of Wuerttemberg was Joseph Suess Oppenheimer, "Jew Suess" of tragic demise. He enjoyed the confidence of the Duke to a high degree and was empowered to carry out radical reforms of the duchy's fiscal system.

The state claimed the sole right to sell some important consumer goods, such as salt, wine, and tobacco, and then farmed out these monopolies, collecting considerable profits. Official positions, too, were often sold to the highest bidder, and this inevitably led to abuses. As an influential favorite, Oppenheimer was bound to have enemies at court. But since he, like many of his Christian contemporaries in similarly privileged positions, loved pleasure and luxury, he enabled his enemies to stir up envy of "the Jew" and to circulate the most outlandish tales about his black magic. When the Duke, his protector, died, Suess Oppenheimer was arrested, tortured, and sentenced to die on the gallows. After sentence had been pronounced, he was asked to convert to Christianity, but he replied proudly, "I want to die a Jew; I am the victim of injustice and oppression."

One of the charges against Suess Oppenheimer was that he had facilitated the entry of Jewish merchants into Wuerttemberg and leased profitable monopolies to several of them. To the Christians of that era this may have been a crime. But actually it bespoke a certain high-mindedness in the Jews who had gained influence and status. They had not forgotten their co-religionists languishing in the ghettos, but rather had done everything in their power to put them on the road to freedom. The Court Jews thus became active participants in the final liberation.

Revolution and Emancipation

In 1781, two years after Lessing's *Nathan the Wise* had depicted Jews, Christians, and Moslems in the light of pure humanity, a book entitled *About the Civic Advancement of the Jews* appeared in Berlin. Its author, Wilhelm Dohm, also a friend of Moses Mendelssohn, lashed out at the injustice with which the Jews had been treated. He showed that the faults for which they were often criticized were but the result of their having been oppressed and outlawed for so long. He also showed that their alleged hostility toward Christians was the response to centuries of persecution. He maintained that, once granted civil rights, Jews would prove to be loyal citizens.

Mirabeau, one of the champions of the French Revolution, translated part of Dohm's book into French, and its impact was first felt in the early stormy days of the revolution. On August 22, 1789, the National Assembly in Paris, while debating the "Declaration of Human and Civil Rights," discussed the question of tolerance. A Conservative deputy wanted Catholicism to be recognized as the official religion and the others to be "tolerated."

Mirabeau leaped to the rostrum and shouted with noble passion:

Official religion! This symbol of despotism must be erased from our legislation! For if you allow this concept to exist in the realm of religion you will have to recognize it also in other areas. You will have an official philosophy and other official systems. This must never happen! Justice alone must reign. The highest principle is the right of the individual—and everything else must be subordinated to it.

In response to these and other brave declarations, the article of the Constitution regarding freedom of conscience was phrased as follows: "No one shall suffer restrictions for his beliefs, even if of a religious nature, as long as their expression does not injure the legally established social order." This article of the Constitution was, however, put into practice only two years later, when on September 28, 1791, the National Assembly issued a decree revoking all special ordinances against the Jews. Upon taking the oath of citizenship they became full citizens of the French state. This example was sooner or later emulated by all European states. Emancipation did not progress without reverses and the appearance of new obstacles, yet it proved to be irrevocable. A new chapter in the history of the Jews had begun.

10

Perpetuation of Judaism Versus Assimilation

The New Freedom and Its Problems

Before the emancipation the Jews had lived in partly voluntary, partly enforced isolation. They had been regarded as strangers, and no one had taken offense at their special rituals and their language, with its Hebrew admixture. With the coming of the Enlightenment and emancipation, the Jews for the first time had to ask themselves whether and to what extent they should adapt to the new way of life of their host nations, and whether they, whose traditions had surrounded their lives as with a fence, should enter the new era with these traditions intact. As long as the world around them had persecuted and rejected them, their refuge and their pride had been the Torah and the Talmud. However, the spirit of the times—in which Lessing wrote *Nathan the Wise* and Herder taught that every man should develop his humanity, a humanity which makes brothers of all peoples regardless of their language and belief— was bound to have a great attraction for the Jews. They had to ask themselves how far they could be receptive to these ideas without becoming disloyal to themselves. The era of enlightenment and emancipation brought many questions for the Jews, and their answers were not uniform. We can gain an idea of the practical difficulties posed by the transition from a letter written by a cultured and wealthy Berlin Jew to a merchant in the province of Glogau, who had asked him to lodge his son in Berlin so that he might study the Talmud in the morning and go to a Christian business school in the afternoon:

You want to send your son to Berlin so that he may spend a good half of the day with Reb Meir of Simche or some other teacher and in the afternoon he is to go to a Christian school? This is not possible. Each of these institutions offers a completely different and conflicting outlook on life. . . . He will spend his mornings weeping and wailing about the Christians, crying "Look down from the Heavens, O Lord, and see how we have become a mockery to the people, are regarded like sheep who are led to the slaughter, to be killed and destroyed, to be beaten and insulted." And in the afternoon he is supposed to learn that we live under wise government where everyone is equal before the law, where the lowest laborer has the same rights as the prince and must not be oppressed. In the morning he is to learn what rules he must follow if perchance he finds leavened bread in his pantry during Passover and, if so, how this sin is to be atoned for, and in the afternoon he will learn that all such laws are the products of a sick mind, at which a better informed man will smile or be annoyed. He will be taught that God's will is done only by enlightening the mind and serving one's fellow men. Which of these doctrines is the young man to follow? Of which is he to approve? To which form of study is he to devote his time and strength?

The writer of this letter, David Friedlaender, undoubtedly overestimated the benevolence of the Christian environment. There were yet many instances of the Jews' being insulted, and equal rights before the law were not enforced until at least half a century later. But this letter clearly illustrates the collision of the two worlds. Would a balance be established—and how?

Moses Mendelssohn, too, had been confronted by these questions. He made one of the foremost contributions to the Jews' adaptation to their German surroundings by translating the Hebrew Bible into German for his co-religionists. He had it printed in Hebrew letters, as most of the Jews of his time had learned to read only Hebrew script. This was the first step towards the use of the German language in the synagogue services. Another important result was that the Jews, one generation after their liberation from the ghetto, spoke pure German.

Yet Mendelssohn never succumbed to the temptation of rejecting the faith of his fathers, even though he suffered under the anti-Semitic utterances. In one of his letters he described what occurred when he went for a walk with his wife and children:

One of my innocent children asked: "What is that boy calling us? Why are they throwing stones at us? What have we done to them?" —"Yes, dearest Papa," another one said, "they are always running after us in the streets calling: 'Jews, Jews!' Is it a crime to be a Jew? What does it matter to them?"—I lowered my eyes and sighed to myself: "Oh, what have human beings allowed to come to pass?"

In his exchange of letters with the outstanding men of his time, Mendelssohn always made it clear that he believed in the basic tenets of his religion. He maintained that the fundamentals of Judaism were essentially rational, but he acknowledged that it remained a mystery why the small nation of the twelve tribes had been entrusted at Mount Sinai with the special task of remaining true to the Covenant with God and to themselves until the end of recorded time.

Baptism, "the Price of Admission to European Culture"

While Mendelssohn himself remained loyal to his faith, his children considered Judaism only a forerunner of a universal, rational religion of humanity, of which Christianity would also become a part. Their decision to convert was all the easier because it was the means of complete access to the advantages of European culture. Mendelssohn's daughter Dorothea at first became a Protestant, as this seemed to her to be "the religion of culture." Later, under the influence of her husband, Friedrich Schlegel, and the strong impression the cathedral of Cologne made on her, she converted to Catholicism. Moses Mendelssohn's most famous grandson, Felix Mendelssohn-Bartholdy, was baptized as a boy.

Conversions to Christianity were characteristic of the period of emancipation. There were several motives. Many of the cultured and wealthy Jews had frequent social contacts with Christian families. At times the *salons* in Jewish houses, such as that of Rachel Levin and Henriette Hertz, became meeting places for the educated men of Berlin. The Protestant theologian Friedrich Schleiermacher has left us a vivid description in one of his letters:

It is very understandable that young scholars and men about town frequent the great Jewish houses here, because they are by far the wealthiest bourgeois families, in fact almost the only ones who keep an open house where one can meet people from all countries and from all walks of life. If one wishes to enjoy good company in informal surroundings one tries to get an introduction to these houses, where everyone with any talent—even if it is only a talent for being sociable —is welcome. He will certainly not be bored because the Jewish ladies are exquisitely educated, while their husbands are forced to take up business at too early an age. They are able to converse on any subject and usually are proficient in one or the other of the arts.

In their contact with their Christian neighbors the Jews found the dietary laws to be an impediment. Anyone who wanted to eat only kosher food could not dine in a Christian house. Keeping the Sabbath and the custom of daily prayer became more and more difficult in an environment which grew more worldly day by day. It must be remembered that among the Christian denominations, too, orthodoxy was giving way to a more liberal outlook. Many biblical and talmudic precepts, such as wearing phylacteries and fringes or beards and sidelocks, and fasting for numerous days, came to be experienced as a meaningless nuisance. Baptism, which no longer carried any special obligations, was a means of escaping this burden.

Added to this was the fact that equal civil rights were still only a partial reality and the Jews frequently still met with considerable obstacles in their attempts to advance. For example, they were now free to study at the universities, but when they had acquired their law degrees they were refused admission to the bar or the bench. This condition of semi-emancipation held dangers which a Jewish writer of those years described as follows:

I am not afraid of times of general adversity, because then those who are suffering work together like oxen under the yoke. Nor am I afraid of the times when liberty is universal. . . . Only those times are dangerous when oppression is relaxed but not completely lifted, when liberty is near but not fully within our grasp. In such times the abandonment of our fathers' customs is considered honorable and advantageous and the enjoyment of the fleeting moment robs eternity of interest.

At that time Heinrich Heine coined the phrase that baptism is "the price of admission to European culture." He himself was baptized in order to reap its advantages, but like many others he could find no true home in the new faith. On the deepest level of their consciousness these converts remained Jews. Heine, the gifted poet who gave the German people some of their best-loved songs, soon regretted his conversion. During his long illness he acquired a new understanding of the Old Testament. The history of the Jewish people evoked his deepest respect. "Our fathers were a gallant people, they humbled themselves before God and could therefore be stiff-necked and defiant towards the powers on earth. . . ."

Rachel Levin, one of the most interesting and important Jewish women of that time, was baptized at the age of forty-six, believing that humanity and Christianity were the same. But in the hour of her death she acknowledged that she was a refugee from the land of Egypt and Canaan and identified herself with the history of her people.

Some other converts took different paths: Friedrich Julius Stahl became a firm adherent of the Protestant church and also the founder of conservative political thought. Karl Marx, whose father had him baptized as a child, turned against all religions and became the apostle of communism, with the promise of salvation in this world rather than the next.

The Christian Reaction

The emancipation of the Jews was supported by many liberal-minded Christians; in fact, the emancipation would have been unthinkable without the change of heart created by the Enlightenment. But this alone could not extinguish centuries of anti-Jewish feeling, which received, moreover, a new impetus when the ghettos were opened.

The attitude of the Christians suddenly changed. They had pitied the Jewish strangers in the ghetto and felt that they were being treated unjustly. What is more, the overwhelming majority of Christians had met them face to face only rarely. But once the Jews began to live among the Christians and to be accorded as well as to demand equal rights, their peculiarities of language and dress became noticeable and were used to arouse suspicion and disapproval. In addition, their Christian fellow citizens were filled with envy when they saw that many of the peddlers from the ghetto, hitherto penned up and despised, had now become prosperous.

The Jews' economic rise was certainly not due to any supernatural talents, let alone unethical practices. It stemmed rather from the fact that about that time all over Europe the state ceased to exercise guardianship over the economy and the guilds relaxed their pusillanimous restrictions on private initiative. The era of economic liberalism had begun. Henceforward everyone was to be the architect of his own fortune, to produce and trade, buy and sell as he saw fit. Competition was to be open, assuring survival of the fittest. The brisk wind of economic freedom swept through the hitherto unruffled world of the guild artisans, whose comfortable standard of living had been guaranteed by protection from competition. But the Jews had never enjoyed this protection. Always segregated, they had usually had to make ends meet under the harshest possible conditions. Hence they were much better suited to the new way of economic life. Who could hold it against them that they took advantage of their opportunity?

Their fellow citizens' envy was exacerbated by a false patriotism born in the wake of the German wars of liberation against Napoleon. After the victory over Napoleon the "patriots" turned against the alleged "inner enemy," the Jews, and thus from 1815 on a number of vile outrages took place, in which students played a leading and inglorious role. As in the Middle Ages, Jewish homes were broken into, the owners mistreated and often put to flight, and these misdeeds were accompanied by the battle cry "Hep, hep!" The origin of this insult is not clear; some trace it back to the initials of the Latin saying *Hierusaleme est perdita* ("Jerusalem is lost").

These hate campaigns were the harbinger of a general political relapse. In every field Jewish emancipation more or less came to a standstill. Only with the approach of new revolutionary storms around the middle of the nineteenth century did the Jews succeed in obtaining their full civil rights.

Nation or Religious Community?

Gabriel Riesser, of Hamburg, was one of his people's most indefatigable champions. A highly gifted jurist, he found after completing his studies that he was excluded from both a legal and an academic career. This snub hurt him deeply, and he determined to become the spokesman for the emancipation of his people.

His main point of attack was the favorite argument of his enemies—that the Jews were not only a religious community but a people unto themselves. This question had already played a role in Napoleon's legislation concerning the Jews. His Minister of Religious Affairs had said in an opinion:

The Jewish religion is to enjoy every freedom guaranteed by our laws. However, the Jews represent not so much a religious community as a people; they live among all nations without intermingling with them. The Government was forced to take into account the eternal character of this people, a people that has survived into our time through all the upheavals and catastrophes of centuries and that by virtue of its religion and its ethos possesses one of the greatest privileges: to have God himself as its lawgiver.

It is difficult to decide whether sarcasm or reverence inspired the author. But most assuredly he touched upon one of the great secrets of Jewish survival. Beyond all doubt, the Covenant with God at Mount Sinai established the Jews not only as a religious community but also as a people. Throughout the eighteen centuries of the dispersion, Jews had always remained both. Moses Mendelssohn, for instance, spoke quite openly of belonging to the Jewish people.

Gabriel Riesser, on the other hand, passionately insisted that the Jews were not separatists. All they were asking was freedom of conscience, the right to profess their ancestral religion. Nobody, he maintained, could at one and the same time belong to two nations or be a citizen of two states:

What other state [besides the German] demands our allegiance? What other fatherland calls upon us for its defense? To reproach us that our ancestors immigrated a hundred or a thousand years ago is inhuman and nonsensical. We did not immigrate, we are native Germans, and because we are, we have no claim to any other homeland; we are either Germans or we are men without a country.

Riesser closes with these words:

We want to belong to the German fatherland, wherever we are. It may demand everything from us it demands from its citizens: we shall willingly sacrifice everything to it—but neither faith nor loyalty, neither truth nor honor; for Germany's heroes and Germany's sages have *not* taught that one becomes a German through such sacrifices.

These fervent words set the tone that was to determine the attitude of the overwhelming majority of the German Jews—until that moment when the nation to which they felt themselves so closely bound brutally turned on them and delivered them to destruction.

Religious Reform

Riesser lived to see his struggle come to a victorious conclusion. He had the satisfaction of being elected a Deputy to the National Assembly in Frankfurt in 1848 and to be appointed the first Jewish judge in Germany.

The struggle for full equality went hand in hand with the efforts of a segment of the Jewish religious community to leave the "ghetto within" by relaxing the ritual laws in order to become fully integrated with their fellow German citizens. Outside pressure frequently affected these internal debates. In fact, the grant of civil rights was in part made dependent on the elimination from the Jewish ritual of everything that could further "national segregation." In other cases, however, the Christian authorities interfered in the opposite sense. Thus, in Prussia, Jewish religious services in German instead of Hebrew were at times forbidden. King William

III was such a determined enemy of liberalism that he only tolerated either traditional Jews or converts.

In contrast to Luther's and Calvin's Reformation, the Jewish reform efforts did not concern themselves with questions of the true faith, but rather with religious practice and adherence to the Mosaic Law. Among the first reforms were the introduction of sermons and of prayers and hymns in German in addition to abbreviated Hebrew versions. Another innovation was the use of the organ in the service as well as the confirmation of girls (until then, only the boy of thirteen had become a *Bar Mitzvah,* a "son of religious commandment"). In some reform congregations the Sabbath was shifted from Saturday to Sunday.

The orthodox opposition to reform was based upon the conviction that the traditional religious practices were God-given and not subject to change by whim or for the sake of accommodation. The hallowing of daily life through the observation of religious laws could well be reconciled with national citizenship and need not prevent Jews from being Germans in Germany and Frenchmen in France.

Since Judaism has no central authority that can make binding decisions, the congregations were always free to decide whether they wanted to join the reform movement or adhere to the traditional ritual. Hence, reform and traditional synagogues existed side by side in many localities.

Emancipation and Democratic Traditions

The history of the Jews in the nineteenth century shows that emancipation met with the fewest obstacles in those countries where vigorous liberal and democratic traditions already existed. That was true particularly in England, the Netherlands, and the Scandinavian countries.

Yet, even in England, Baron Lionel de Rothschild—elected to Parliament by the City of London district—had to wait a number of years before Parliament decided to modify the oath which every member had to swear on the Bible "according to the true Christian faith." Only then could he take his seat. Benjamin Disraeli, too, had intervened in the dispute over the parliamentary oath. He had been converted to Christianity in his youth, yet he distinguished himself by always proudly acknowledging his Jewish descent. Queen Victoria, whose special favor he enjoyed, made him Lord Beaconsfield, and his great influence as leader of the Conservative Party and repeatedly as Prime Minister probably helped materially to strengthen the position of British Jewry.

But above all the Jews benefited by the spirit of civil liberty, the pride in democratic rights, and the national self-confidence in the countries mentioned above. Ludwig Boerne, who had grown up in the Frankfurt ghetto, had quite rightly discerned that German hatred of the Jews was nourished by the outdated, rigid caste system. "The poor Germans!" he had written in 1832. "They live on the ground floor, oppressed by the higher orders on the seven floors above them, and it makes them feel so much better to talk of the people who live in the basement. Though they cannot be Privy Councilors, at least they are not Jews." Such consolation was unnecessary in countries where the enjoyment of equal rights was more deeply rooted and whose society was more mobile and open, and distributed opportunities on an equal basis.

11

Anti-Semitism

Those who had hoped that the spirit of freedom, of tolerance and enlightenment, would progress without hindrance to "overcome the resistance of a callous world" were forced to realize that the accumulated poison of many centuries could not be flushed out so easily from hearts and minds. This became evident toward the end of the century of emancipation in frightening outbreaks of a renewed hatred for Jews, which was now called "anti-Semitism" and was based on the pseudoscientific racial theory.

Reaction and Pogroms in Russia

Yet it would be wrong to assume that by then the greater part of Jewry had actually come to enjoy the blessings of emancipation. The third partition of Poland had resulted in bringing almost two million Polish Jews under Russian rule, and thus the majority of European Jews now lived under the sway of the Czar. But their emancipation was far from the thoughts of the "Emperor of all the Russians," who rather sought to "improve" and convert them.

One of the chief means of this policy was to extend conscription for the Jews, without in return granting them any rights or alleviating their position. On the contrary, conscription for the Jews took a much more severe form, beginning with minors at the age of twelve. (At that time Russians were conscripted for a term of twenty-five years.) The nobility and the well-to-do merchants and artisans were exempted—and originally this had also applied to Jews. Apart from these classes, every district had to supply a certain quota of recruits. The recruiting of Jews was entrusted to officials of the Jewish community, a hated duty which divided the

Jews against themselves and exacerbated the contrast between rich and poor. Jewish residence was confined to western *gouvernements;* but for military duty the Jewish conscripts were transported into the far-eastern parts of the country in order to separate them from their co-religionists and to "encourage" their conversion. The misery of the families thus separated from their sons was heart-breaking. The conscripts were mourned as if they were dead. Before every levy the hapless victims took flight and often escaped into the forests. They were pursued, and if not enough adult Jews could be rounded up, the chase for the minors began. The Russian authorities increased the pressure by simply taking along the responsible community elders if the required number of conscripts could not be found. In the barracks everything was done to make it impossible for the Jews to observe their rituals, and they were tormented in all kinds of ways to force them into conversion. Many finally gave in to their torturers; others resolutely bore a martyrdom of many years. The sufferings of the under-age conscripts, among whom were many children aged eight to ten, were unimaginable. The famous Russian revolutionary Alexander Herzen described how he once met such a transport:

There they were standing, pale, emaciated and frightened in their heavy, ill-fitting soldier's coats with the stiff, stand-up collars. With helpless eyes, appealing for mercy, they looked up to the garrison soldiers who were roughly lining them up; and the blue circles under their eyes were evidence of fever and ague. Thus the poor children, deprived of all love and care . . . marched toward their graves.

As if the shadow cast over the lives of the Russian Jews by the cruelties of conscription was not enough, deep-seated superstition, coupled with greed, again and again led to the tribulations of looting, wanton destruction, and massacre. These outbreaks of popular fury were called pogroms. As in the Middle Ages, they were often occasioned by accusing the Jews of ritual murder. The authorities frequently remained so passive that the masses believed that the Czar was in favor of these acts of "revenge." The belief gained even more ground after the assassination of Czar Alexander II in 1881, for which the Jews were falsely blamed.

What happened during such pogroms was described by an investigating commission:

The riots began again around seven o'clock in the morning on April 16, spreading like wildfire through the entire town. Store clerks, hostlers, coachmen, artisans, footmen, officer's batmen, soldiers, all of them joined the riot. The town presented an unusual picture: The streets were covered with goose down and broken furniture, doors and windows were smashed; a rampaging mob pouring forth in every direction, shouting and screaming, continued to work its destruction without hindrance; the picture was completed by the utter indifference of the non-Jewish inhabitants in the face of the mad havoc of destruction. . . . Toward evening the riots increased in violence as in the meantime peasants from the surrounding country had poured into the town, intent on their share of Jewish loot. . . .

In the synagogues the Torah rolls were torn up and trampled into the dirt. Frequently the pogroms found their climax in arson and other such crimes.

In the subsequent court hearings the "agitators" received negligible sentences as if they had merely been guilty of gross misdemeanor. This confirmed the Christian population in its belief that nothing was to be feared from a pogrom, but much to be gained. During a pogrom in Melitopol a seven-year-old peasant girl wandering through the town was asked what she was doing there. Her grandmother, she said, had told her, "I hear they are going to beat up the Jews in town; why don't you go and bring me back a little kerchief."

The constant threat of pogroms brought two million Jewish refugees to the United States.

The So-Called Racial Doctrine

The western world was horrified by the pogroms. They were attributed to the ignorance and political backwardness of the Russian people. But at the same time, in the countries that considered themselves progressive, a racial "theory" was developing which clothed the old "Judaeophobia" with the mantle of scientific truth and far surpassed it in its terrible consequences.

This doctrine originated in the natural sciences. Darwin had traced the origin of species in the animal world to the "struggle for existence," according to which the strong, well-adapted species survives, while the weak, poorly-adapted species becomes extinct. Thus one began to classify human beings into various subspecies called "races," a concept which had formerly been employed only in the breeding of animals. Since no acknowledged standards existed for these classifications, each scientist established his own. One spoke of three races, another of five, a third of twenty and more races and subraces.

If these scientists had confined themselves to the enumeration of physical characteristics, their doctrines would have remained harmless. But they maintained that physical characteristics were invariably linked to certain mental and psychological traits. Thus a French writer, Count Arthur Gobineau, proclaimed those peoples which philologists had classed as "Aryans" because of the similarity of their languages, to be a special race. He maintained that only this race had creative abilities, that it was high-spirited, bold, and idealistic. He contended that it was superior to other human races because of its intelligence and energy and the incomparably higher moral stage of development it supposedly had reached. Of the Negroes he wrote:

The black variety is the simplest one; it occupies the lowest rung of the ladder. That it is more closely related to the animals is proved by the shape of its pelvis which determines its character from the moment of conception. Intellectually it can never progress beyond narrow limits. And yet the Negro, with his narrow . . . brow and the signs of brute physical violence in the center of his skull is not exactly an animal.

Herder had still objected to the application of the concept of race to human beings by the scientists of his time. But in Gobineau's time the dignity of man was no longer held in such high esteem.

His assertions found a wide echo because they flattered the vanity of the Europeans, who were then about to establish their hegemony all over the world. The scientific value of his notions was nil. Nobody has ever been able to prove that the millions of members of one race have the same mental and psychological characteristics. Indisputably, there are everywhere clever and stupid, lazy and industrious, courageous and cowardly people. This is evident even within the small circle of a family, whose members may yet bear a strong physical resemblance to each other.

Since the racial classifications were left entirely to the discretion of the individual scientist, it was not long before the assertion was made that the Jews were a special race, which by virtue of its segregation had maintained itself in a particularly pure form. They were considered a branch of the "Semitic race," which inhabits Syria, Arabia, and Egypt. But at the same time they were distinguished from these Semitic peoples, for "anti-Semitism"—the word was used for the first time in 1879—was aimed by no means at the Arabs or the Egyptians, but exclusively against the Semites of Jewish origin. This was clear proof that the entire "racial doctrine" was merely a pretext for dressing up ancient religious hostility in a more up-to-date fashion. A glance at the history of the Jews exposes the complete folly of this "doctrine": In the eighth century, the King of the Khazars, a Slavic tribe, and many of his followers, had been converted to Judaism. The descendants of these Jews were certainly not Semites; but to the extent that they adhered to the Jewish faith they fell victim to anti-Semitic prejudices.

The Anti-Semitic Delusion

The extent to which the new anti-Semitism was rooted in the old religious hatred of the Jews is clear from its delusions. Its protagonists spoke, not of "the Jews," but of "the Jew," as if he were a demon with supernatural faculties. "The Jew" was taking the place of the medieval devil. He was simultaneously admired, hated, and feared. Although the Jew was no longer accused of poisoning wells, he was now in all seriousness charged with insidiously destroying everything he came in touch with: the "host nation," its culture, its economy, its politics. Just like the devil himself he was held to aim at nothing less than dominion over the whole world. In the anti-Semitic caricatures the Jew bears all the features of the medieval devil.

On the one hand, anti-Semitism thus appealed to ancient instincts: to paranoia and the fear of demons. A typical example is found in a letter by Richard Wagner to King Ludwig II of Bavaria:

... that I consider the Jewish race the natural enemy of all untainted humanity and everything noble in it: that we Germans in particular will perish of it is certain, and perhaps I am the last German who is able to hold his ground against this pervasive Judaism.

On the other hand, anti-Semitism's new biological foundation gave people the feeling that they were the champions of a new "scientific view of life." Moritz Lazarus, an anthropological psychologist and philosopher, was one of the first to recognize that the new hatred for the Jews would ultimately turn also against Christianity. In 1880 he wrote: "Anti-Semitism is anti-Christianity. For Christ the Founder and all his apostles were Jews. This whole theory of blood and race is a product of our grossly materialistic outlook on life."

The metamorphosis of the medieval hatred of the Jews into racial anti-Semitism had still another fateful result. In the Middle Ages the Jews had been able to clear themselves of the "Divine Curse" by conversion. Now the assertion that they constituted an inferior race made them the object of persecution without any possibility of individual vindication. They had been able to confront the old anti-Semitism with proud loyalty to their faith. But the Jew who was persecuted and vilified because of his race had no freedom of choice. He could not opt out of his race; he had been laid under an ineluctable ban. The individual Jew, regardless of his accomplishments—whether a monumental discovery, distinguished cultural achievements, outstanding bravery in war, donating his wealth to charity—remained despised by the anti-Semites. Either the individual Jew was regarded as an exception or his virtues and achievements were considered a mere mask for his essentially evil nature. Hence every Jew encountering an anti-Semite suffered the torments of an innocent outlaw. In his book, *Mein Weg als Jude und Deutscher* ("My Journey as Jew and German"), Jakob Wassermann gave moving expression to his agony:

There is no point in trying to hide. They merely say, "The coward, he hides himself because his bad conscience drives him to it." It is futile to go among them and seek their friendship. There is no point in keeping faith with them, either as comrades-in-arms or as fellow citizens. . . . There is no point in living for them or dying for them. They say: "He is a Jew." . . .

The assertion that the Jews are at one and the same time both inferior and a highly dangerous "race" contained the terrible inference that this "focus of infection" could be fought neither by education or conversion, nor by suitable social or political measures. Hence very early we come upon references in the writings of the fanatical anti-Semites to the necessity of "liquidating" or "exterminating" the Jews, as if they were not human beings but noxious bacteria or vermin. These thinkers had reached a moral nadir which sixty years later led to unspeakable deeds.

The Dreyfus Affair

The first great anti-Semitic outbreak occurred in France. One major instance began in 1894, when Captain Alfred Dreyfus, a Jew, was accused of handing over secret documents to a German officer. The accusation rested solely on the similarity of Dreyfus' handwriting to that of a letter that had been removed from a wastebasket in German Embassy. No motive could be found; Dreyfus lived in very comfortable circumstances. Only three out of five experts maintained that his handwriting was identical with that of the letter. But a court martial sentenced him to penal servitude for life on Devil's Island. The verdict was, moreover, based on secret documents which the War Minister submitted to the judge without allowing the defendant access to them—a clear violation of the law.

The real reason for convicting Dreyfus was that he was a Jew and that the French General Staff was greatly interested in making him the scapegoat in this unpleasant affair. The press of the radical right at once launched the most outrageous anti-Semitic tirades. For almost twelve years anti-Semitism raged in France like a virulent disease; it took that long before Dreyfus' innocence was established and he was acquitted and reinstated in the army with full honors.

A coincidence led to the review of the verdict. A colonel in the French Counter-Intelligence, Georges Picquart, came across the draft of a letter which had also been purloined from the German Embassy. It was addressed to a French officer, Major Esterhazy, who at that time was applying for a position in Counter-Intelligence. Picquart discovered that Esterhazy's handwriting was identical with that of the fateful document that had sent Dreyfus to Devil's Island. He was convinced that Dreyfus was innocent and that Esterhazy (who gambled, played the stock market, and was up to his ears in debt) was the traitor. He informed the Chief of the General Staff of his discovery and demanded that the case be reopened. He was told that the honor of the French Officer Corps would not permit it. But Picquart, a knight *sans peur et sans reproche,* was not satisfied, and followed the voice of his conscience. He handed over to a lawyer all his material.

Thus began the fight for release of an innocent man. In its course Picquart was arrested and dismissed from the French army. But later, together with Dreyfus, he was reinstated with full honors; eventually he became Minister of War. The machinations of the army in its attempts to suppress the truth were scandalous, while the anti-Semitic press equated patriotism with hatred of the Jews and stopped at nothing in inciting the public. The mob cried, "Death to the Jews!" and destroyed Jewish stores and workshops. All the more admirable was the courage of a number of outstanding Frenchmen who took Picquart's side and considered it a matter of national honor to obtain justice for Dreyfus. The most famous of them was the writer Emile Zola, whose Open Letter to the President of the Republic, with its ten-times-repeated *"J'accuse!"* had an immense effect.

During those years France was to split into two camps, the "Dreyfusards," who fought for justice and humanity, and the "anti-Dreyfusards" (some of them leaders in French Christianity), who unfurled the tainted banner of anti-Semitism. Wherever in those days Frenchmen met they immediately took sides. The very scope and passion of the public debate finally rid most of the French people of the poison of anti-Semitism. When, in 1906, Dreyfus was made a Chevalier of the Legion of Honor, the ceremony took place in the presence of cheering crowds.

The Birth of Zionism

The Dreyfus trial had far-reaching consequences. Among the journalists who had come to Paris to report the trial was Theodor Herzl, an Austrian Jew. He had grown up in a liberal, largely assimilated family, but his encounter with the vicious outbreaks of anti-Semitism, which he had considered a thing of the past, revolutionized his views. He realized that the Jews were a defenseless minority that could time and again be victimized whenever there was a need for scapegoats.

Everywhere we have loyally striven to merge with the national communities among which we lived, only retaining the faith of our fathers. But we are prevented from doing so. . . . In our native countries, in which we have dwelled for centuries, we are despised as aliens; often by those whose forefathers were not even in the country when our forefathers were already suffering there. In vain we are everywhere loyal patriots. . . . If we were left in peace . . . . But I believe we'll never be left in peace.

These experiences led Herzl to the conclusion that the Jews must again establish a state of their own. His views coincided with a group that had even earlier demanded the return of the Jews to Zion, to Palestine; he became its intellectual leader and tireless champion. As early as 1897 the "Zionists" convened their first congress in Basel. Until his death, in 1904, Herzl was constantly traveling in order to gain friends for his cause among the sovereigns of Europe. At the same time the Zionists began to buy land in Palestine, which was settled and cultivated by Jewish emigrants, who came especially from Russia. When, thirty years after Herzl's death, anti-Semitism began its reign of terror in Germany, thousands of persecuted Jews found a refuge in Palestine. On August 17, 1949, a little more than a year after the State of Israel was established, Theodor Herzl's remains were transferred to Jerusalem in solemn ceremony. Every year hundreds of young Israelis make the pilgrimage to this memorial. They are citizens of a country where they can hold their heads up and where no one can insult them because of their faith, their nationality, their heritage.

Anti-Semitism and Nationalism in Germany

At about the same time that French nationalism combined forces with anti-Semitism, German nationalists, too, turned toward this evil ally. Their national unity having been attained relatively late, in 1871, the Germans still felt insecure as a nation. They also felt that as latecomers they had been shortchanged in the distribution of colonies and spheres of influence. All the more did the German nationalists feel impelled to spur German self-esteem. Geibel's words *Am deutschen Wesen soll die Welt genesen* ("The German spirit shall save the world") became the battle cry of these groups. But what was that German spirit? It was difficult to define the concept—and much simpler to focus on the picture that anti-Semitism painted of the Jew. For Paul de Laguarde, one of the most influential apostles of anti-Semitic nationalism, it was the Jews who had so far prevented the Germans from being true to themselves. The Jew, he said, makes it impossible for the German people "to fulfill its manifest destiny." The conclusion could only be "Throw out all the Jews who demand the right to exist in Germany as Jews." (The Jews constituted 0.8 per cent of the German population.) In the *Prussian Yearbooks* the famous historian Heinrich von Treitschke wrote articles under the heading "A Word about our Jews," in which he coined the fateful saying, "The Jews are our undoing," and, like de Laguarde, conjured up the danger of Germany's "alienization."

About the same time the Berlin Court Chaplain, Adolf Stoecker, discovered that political capital could be made out of anti-Semitism. Originally he wanted to oppose the Socialist labor movement with a Christian workers' organization. When his campaigns among the Berlin workers met with little success, he adopted anti-Semitic slogans and began to draw sizable crowds from the ranks of the petite bourgeoisie and the impoverished middle class.

In both cases the usefulness of anti-Semitism is evident. In the case of de Laguarde and his successors in the so-called *Alldeutschen Verein* ("Pan-German League") the Jew as the alleged "inner enemy" was used to stir up nationalist sentiments. Stoecker's success was based on the fact that the middle classes were under pressure from both sides: on the one hand they had to defend themselves against the competition of big capital (the hated department stores, for instance), while on the other hand they would do anything not to become "submerged" in the proletariat. Hence they readily believed that "the Jew" was their real enemy and responsible for both capitalism and socialism. While the workers were not immune to anti-Semitism, they knew perfectly well that in their struggle for a better life their real adversary was the entrepreneur. Thus they could not be taken in by a decoy, and remained largely immune to anti-Semitism. One of their most respected and popular leaders, August Bebel, coined the apt phrase "Anti-Semitism is the socialism of the blockheads."

Perhaps the virus of the anti-Semitic mania could have been expelled from Germany's body politic, as it had been in France, if it also had culminated in a crisis. Instead, the poison continued its work insidiously. Anti-Semitism was now the fashion in nationalist circles. The other parties, while rejecting it, did not take it seriously, and hence its dangers remained unrecognized. Moreover, the Jews themselves did not really feel threatened by it; they considered it an ugly moral disease which, however, attacked only a few fellow citizens.

The first of anti-Semitic violence took place under the Weimar Republic. It should have been recognized as a storm signal, but the worry and unrest of the post-World War I years served as distraction. In June, 1922, Walther Rathenau was murdered by a group of young anti-Semitic fanatics. Not only had he successfully organized Germany's supply of raw materials during World War I, but also he had, as Foreign Minister, concluded the highly successful Treaty of Rapallo with Soviet Russia. As a Jew he had long been the target of anti-Semites, whose brutality was demonstrated in verses like this: "Kill Walther Rathenau, the god-damned Jewish sow!"

This seed bore fruit. One of the three assassins was caught, and in court he recited all the confused balderdash that anti-Semitic propaganda had put in his head. Among other things, he believed that Rathenau was one of the "Elders of Zion," who supposedly had planned a conspiracy against the entire world. A pernicious forgery under this title had just been widely disseminated. Perhaps there would still have been time to unmask the inanities and dangers of anti-Semitism if men and women of all parties and viewpoints had decisively condemned the assassination. But the murder was soon forgotten. The public was preoccupied with the burdens of the Versailles Treaty and the worries engendered by inflation and Communist unrest.

The Flowering of German-Jewish Culture

In spite of these danger signals the prevailing view was that, particularly in Germany, Jewish integration left little to be desired. The Jewish contribution to European and especially German cultural and intellectual life was universally acknowledged; in some cases it had worldwide effects (to list only three names: Karl Marx, Sigmund Freud, and Albert Einstein). Modern political science, psychology, and physics are unthinkable without them, and politics, literature, and technology have been decisively transformed under the influence of their doctrines and discoveries.

No one who knows the history of the Jewish people will find it surprising that the Jews played a large and active role in intellectual life. For centuries they had been called the People of the Book, who began to instruct their sons in the Torah and the Talmud at the age of six. In the years after World War I Jakob Wassermann, Arnold Zweig, Stefan Zweig, Bruno Frank, and Alfred Doeblin wrote their widely read novels and short stories. Joseph Roth, that restless wanderer and incomparable storyteller, raised a moving monument to his eastern Jewish brothers in *Job* and *Juden auf Wanderschaft*. In Prague Franz Kafka, already marked by death, was writing his profound and prophetic novels, which gave rise to a host of interpretations. He became world famous through their English translations. Perhaps Jean-Paul Sartre is right in seeing in Kafka's novel *The Trial* a parable of Jewish fate:

Like the hero of the novel, the Jew is involved in a long trial. He hardly knows his judges and his counsel, he does not know what the charge against him is, and yet he knows that one believes him to be guilty. . . . However magnificent his outward position may appear to be, this endless trial secretly gnaws at him, and as in the novel it may happen that strangers, under the pretext that he has lost his case, pounce upon him, drag him to an unfamiliar suburb and kill him there.

After the fall of the Austro-Hungarian monarchy Hugo von Hofmannsthal wrote his charming comedies in which the skeptical grace of old Vienna has become immortal; he presented the composer Richard Strauss with the world's most glorious opera librettos. Max Reinhardt introduced a new theatrical style in his Shakespeare performances at the *Deutsches Theatre* (the "German Theatre" in Berlin). Actors like Ernst Deutsch, Fritz Kortner, and Elisabeth Bergner moved their audiences to frenzied applause. Arnold Schoenberg was head of the Berlin Conservatory. Conductors like Otto Klemperer and Bruno Walter were honored in concert halls all over the world.

Great critics like Alfred Kerr, Alfred Polgar, and Karl Kraus, endowed with an unerring sense of quality, set high standards for literature and drama. Political journalists like Kurt Tucholsky used their pens like rapiers against smugness and reaction.

Outstanding Jewish scientists were active in almost every field of scientific endeavor. During World War I Fritz Haber had discovered a process of nitrogen fixation which made possible the artificial production of saltpeter (potassium nitrate), indispensable in the manufacture of gunpowder. He received the Nobel Prize for Chemistry in 1919, and until 1933 he was the director of the Kaiser Wilhelm Institute for Physical Chemistry in Berlin. James Franck and Gustav Hertz received the Nobel Prize in 1926 for their experimental confirmation of Niels Bohr's atomic theory (Niels Bohr himself had a Jewish mother). Of thirty-nine Jewish Nobel laureates, twenty-six came from German-speaking countries. All of them increased Germany's reputation in the world. But to the sick minds of the anti-Semites this was a crime.

The Jews' Search for Jewish Relevancy in the Modern World

For the anti-Semites it was unimportant whether a Jew was orthodox, liberal, or completely divorced from his faith. They knew nothing of Judaism as a living force. Instead, they had the most confused and arbitrary ideas; for example, of the Talmud they knew only distorted quotations, cited out of context. Since they despised the intellect, it was of no interest to them that in modern times, too, Judaism had produced philosophers and theologians whose thinking was rooted in their faith and who in masterly interpretations illuminated the self-identification of the modern Jew. Three such thinkers were Franz Rosenzweig, Leo Baeck, and Martin Buber.

Franz Rosenzweig grew up in Kassel, studied medicine, history and philosophy, and received his doctorate with a dissertation about Hegel. At the age of thirty he began an intensive study of the sources of Judaism and submitted to the philosopher Hermann Cohen of the Academy for the *Wissenschaft* of Judaism in Berlin a plan for the regreneration of Jewish education and learning. During World War I Rosenzweig wrote the larger part of his principal work, *Der Stern Der Erloesung* ("The Star of Redemption"), in letters from the front. This book, which appeared in 1921, was a hymnic exegesis of God's redemptive history, and especially of the Kingdom-of-God message of Judaism, which continued to exist side by side with Christianity.

How deeply Rosenzweig was rooted in both his German and Jewish heritages is shown by a letter he wrote to a friend in 1923. He reported about a meeting in Hamburg in which he was asked where he stood: "I refused to answer this question; if Life were one day to put me to the rack and tear me in half, I would of course know which half would contain the heart . . . but I would also know that I would not survive the operation." In the same letter he also said: "Our work will at best be posthumously rewarded by Germany. But we do it nevertheless—as long as we do it in Germany—for Germany." In 1920 Rosenzweig founded the *Freies Judisches Lehrhaus,* an adult Jewish educational institution in Frankfurt. Soon after, he fell seriously ill with sclerosis, which led to his early death in 1929.

Rabbi Leo Baeck, was Rosenzweig's senior by more than ten years. In 1905 he had published *Das Wesen Des Judentums* ("The Essence of Judaism"). The choice of the title showed that it was a reply to the famous essay "The Essence of Christianity" by the celebrated liberal theologian Adolf von Harnack. To illustrate the relationship between Judaism and the doctrines of salvation stemming from it—Christianity, Islam, and communism (which in its essence is secularized messianism)—Baeck coined the following analogy: "A mother never hates her child; but the child forgets and denies its mother." In 1942 he was deported to Terezin, and whenever he "had a blank sheet and a quiet hour" he wrote his thoughts on Jewish life and the Jewish people, which in 1955 were published under the title *This People Israel.* To him the essence of the Jewish people lay in their being different, a difference justified only if accompanied by respect for the rights of all others, and justified also by the tensions which make this people at the same time both the most conservative and the most radical, both the most joyful and the most ascetic. To him the Jews are the people of loyalty:

Perhaps loyalty is the decisive characteristic of this people, as it may be of all mankind. One might say: Just as loyalty is the great reconciliation between I and Thou—between the I and Thou of two human beings—so it is the great conciliator between the I and Thou of groups and nations, the great conciliator of differences and opposites. . . . Loyalty is not based on likeness. It has to stand the test of difference. . . . Thus loyalty creates a unity, the only unity which can truly exist among men. It is the living human contribution to the Covenant, which, as the wonderful, inexhaustible parable says, God has entered into with man. In its lasting, eternal aspect the Covenant is called: Law; in its human aspect, encompassed in time and space, it is called: Loyalty.

Martin Buber was born in Vienna in 1878. From 1924 to 1933 he was Professor for Jewish Religion and Ethics at Frankfurt on Main, and from 1938 until his death in 1965 he taught at the Hebrew University in Jerusalem. He collected the lore and legends of Hasidism and recast them in a modern literary form. Together with Franz Rosenzweig he retranslated the Bible, recreating as faithfully as possible the archaic character of the ancient Hebrew tongue. His philosophical writings, such as *I and Thou* and *Paths in Utopia,* were widely read far beyond his Jewish audience.

Buber's view of God was decisively influenced by his encounter with Hasidism. According to him, God is the true Thou of man. God "speaks to man through the objects and beings He sends into his life; man responds by his dealings with these objects and beings." "Man does not encounter God in order to concern himself with God, but in order to prove that there is meaning in the world. . . . Whoever wants to speak with men without speaking with God, his word is not consummated; but whoever wants to speak with God without speaking with men, his word goes astray." "The greatest achievement of Judaism," said Buber, "is not that it taught the existence of the one true God, who is the origin and goal of all being, but that it showed that man could talk to this God, that he could say Thou to Him, stand face to face with Him, relate himself to Him." In Buber's view, formalized religion contains a deep danger to man, because through it man tries over and over again to make sure of God, to get hold of him, to talk *about* him instead of *to* him. Man wants to hallow the world for God by cult and sacrament, but only too easily secular life and divine worship proceed side by side without ever touching each other. "Whoever divides his life between God and the world by giving the world 'its due,' in order to be able to give God 'His due,' refuses God the required service: to give direction to every endeavor, to consecrate daily living within the world without and the soul within." This is the true significance of the Jew's sober observance of the commandments, which fills his entire working day, from awakening to falling asleep.

12

Anti-Semitism in the New Land*

The Colonial Period

Jewish settlers gradually found their way to each of the thirteen colonies beginning with Virginia in 1621 and reaching Georgia in 1733. One of the first major Jewish settlements in America was established in 1654—just thirty-four years after the pilgrims landed in Plymouth—when a group of twenty-three "poor and healthy" Sephardic Jews landed in New Amsterdam. Coming from Brazil, where they had gone to flee the Spanish Inquisition, they were captured by Spanish pirates and rescued by a French man-of-war, the St. Charles, which brought them to North American shores. When they arrived in New Amsterdam, now New York, the Governor, Peter Stuyvesant, did all in his power to bar from the colony these "hateful enemies and blasphemers of the name of Christ." It might have been a new world but this cruel attitude was very old. The Dutch West India Company refused Peter Stuyvesant permission to expel the Jews from the colony. In unbelief the Governor warned that the admission of Jews would lead to the admission of "Papists and Lutherans." From the very beginning of the Jews' settlement, therefore, this struggle to win acceptance as a free people in this land has also been related to the very same attitudes of mind that would enable America to become a land of religious freedom and equal opportunity.

Fortunately for the Jews not all of the colonies were governed

* This chapter is by Robert H. Roberts and is new in this translation.— EDITOR.

116

by men like Stuyvesant. The American ideals of religious liberty and freedom of conscience had already expressed themselves in some of the early colonies. For instance, Roger Williams fought hard in Rhode Island for complete religious liberty so that the only test of loyalty required was that of obedience to his Majesty's laws. Freedom of conscience in matters pertaining to religion was also incorporated into the Constitution of Pennsylvania in 1682. Quite naturally Newport, Rhode Island, and Philadelphia, Pennsylvania, became early centers of American Jewish life.

Nevertheless, New York City remained a most important center for Jewish Americans. English control of the Dutch possessions in 1664 brought greater religious freedom. Yet because the oath of citizenship in the colony of New York obliged the individual to swear upon "the true faith of a Christian" it was impossible for Jews to become naturalized until 1727. Restrictive measures against the Jews were introduced and enforced in New York. In 1737 the Assembly of New York precluded Jews from voting for members of that body. Jews were also restricted in retail trading, and for them to engage in wholesale commerce required the consent of the Governor.

From the very beginning of Jewish history on these shores one can sense an ambivalence in America's response to them. With one hand America gave and with the other, often very subtly, it took away. These early Jewish settlers made homes in the colonies and quickly found a place for themselves in the life of the New World. Early America was, in many ways, extremely friendly to the Jews. For one thing, Christian theology in the New World was a Puritan theology which emphasized the Hebrew roots of Christianity. The Puritan took the Jewish Bible seriously. In fact, a proposed Seal for the United States, designed by Benjamin Franklin and Thomas Jefferson, showed the Children of Israel crossing the Red Sea and bore the inscription, "Rebellion to Tyrants is Obedience to God."

But the fact remains, anti-Jewish sentiment has not been absent from any period of American history. An overly optimistic view of the status of the Jew in America leads too easily to a dismissal of the long, hard struggle of American Jewry to gain possession of basic human rights.

Regardless of the anti-Jewish feeling, American Jews have from colonial days become fully American and have possessed the aspirations, dreams, and ideals typical of this nation. Indeed, in the American Revolution the American Jewish response was typical of that of their fellow countrymen. Some were Loyalists, but the vast majority were committed to the American patriotic cause. Jewish soldiers fought in the ranks of the Revolutionary Army and rose to positions of leadership as commissioned officers.

Notable strides towards religious freedom were taken with the signing of the great documents of liberty. These documents, of importance to all Americans, were of special significance to the Jews in the light of centuries of persecution and discrimination. The Declaration of Independence signed on July 4, 1776, declared it self-evident that all men are created equal and endowed with certain inalienable rights. The Constitution of the United States of America ratified by the States in 1790 stipulated that no religious test should be required as a qualification to public office or public trust in the United States. A year later the first amendment forbade Congress to make any law respecting a religious establishment or prohibiting free exercise of religious practices. Theoretically the Jews obtained a place of equality with their fellow citizens. Some of the states, however, were slow to implement the intent of these statements of liberty and freedom. It was not until 1826 that legislation was passed in the State of Maryland to extend to Jews the same privileges and freedoms enjoyed by Christians.

The Early Nineteenth-Century Immigrations

Events in Germany were beginning to trigger a major immigration to the United States. From 1820 to 1880, the Jewish population swelled from less than 10,000 to 275,000. These newly American Jews were part of a great wave of immigration that included 7,000,000 Christians. This immigration came at a time when the burgeoning economy of the United States required workers to open up unclaimed territory. These workers contributed in turn to an expanding economy by creating demands for businessmen, traders, and peddlers. For the most part the Christian refugees, mostly of German peasant stock, filled the demand for the labor force. The

Jewish refugees generally became the small entrepreneurs. The Jewish trader or peddler carried his merchandise to the pioneer families and established businesses in the thousands of villages, towns, and small cities that began to emerge. In fact, some of America's great department stores are the outgrowth of the efforts of these early Jewish peddlers. The Jews of this 1820–80 immigration wave did not cluster in the cities of the East, but scattered throughout the country. They entered into every area of American life. When their numbers were sufficient, they formed synagogues.

The Civil War Era

During the Civil War Jews in the North wore the Union blue while those in the South donned the Confederate grey. Like all other American religious groups they were divided over the issue of slavery. Rabbis in the northern states urged the abolition of slavery and called for Jews to support and fight for the Union. Their counterparts in the South urged similar support for the Confederacy. Thousands of Jews fought on both sides. August Bondi, one of the earliest settlers in Kansas, was an outspoken opponent of slavery who served valiantly in the Union Army. On the other hand, former United States Senator from Louisiana, Judah P. Benjamin, was both Secretary of State and Secretary of War in the southern Cabinet.

Throughout the nineteenth century the predominant object of prejudice in Protestant America was the Roman Catholic, not the Jew. The Roman Catholic Church, which was growing rapidly due to immigration, operated in the face of mounting chronic opposition. This opposition was expressed in such groups as the militantly anti-Catholic Native American Association, which was organized to oppose easy naturalization of the Irish and the Germans. There followed the Know-Nothing Party, which was of considerable political importance prior to 1860. Convinced that the Roman Catholic Church was the agent through which foreign powers were attempting to control the United States, the Know-Nothing movement, through propaganda and political manipulation, sought to maintain a monolithic Protestant America and to hold back the natural development of pluralism. Curbing Catholic immigration and fostering increased Protestant influence in the public schools were its two major goals.

Such bigoted attitudes towards Catholics naturally stimulated hatred and suspicion of Jews. The nativists liked to talk about "original American stock" and were highly suspicious of deviant modes of behavior that might be considered foreign. Anti-Catholic sentiment often included derogatory remarks about Jews. These feelings were verbalized when the American Party's candidate for President in 1856, Millard Fillmore, charged that his Republican opponent, John C. Fremont, "was a Jew educated in the Mosaic faith." This tactic was an attempt to divert attention from the issue of slavery by whipping up feeling against immigrants.

This rising tide of sentiment against the Jew as a foreigner was manifested during the Civil War. Due to spreading rumors that Jewish traders were responsible for the shortage of supplies, General Ulysses Grant on December 17, 1862, ordered Jews expelled from the lines. Grant was later to apologize for this incident. Ironically Jews in the South were also being blamed for the lack of supplies.

Also during the Civil War, Congress established a chaplain's corps for the Union Army. In order to qualify as a chaplain the clergyman had to be a regularly ordained Christian minister. Pressure was immediately put upon President Lincoln for an amendment which would allow for non-Christian chaplains. At Lincoln's request, Congress concurred, despite many Christian voices that denounced the action.

By 1877 evidence of the gathering momentum of anti-Jewish feeling was revealed by the refusal of the Grand Union Hotel in Saratoga to permit Joseph Seligman, a New York banker, and his family to register. The incident received national attention and pointed up the growing restrictive measures that were being brought to bear against the Jews in attempts to keep them out of schools, neighborhoods, resort clubs, public lodging, and colleges.

The Second Wave of Immigration

At that moment, when the rising tide of anti-Jewish feeling became evident, America welcomed to its shores a new wave of

22,000,000 immigrants. Between 1881 and 1924 at least 2,000,000 new Jewish Americans arrived on these shores. These orthodox immigrants, strikingly different from the Jews they found in America, were penniless. Different though the newcomers were in customs, tradition, and theology, the Jewish community of America responded to their needs through a network of organizations geared to helping them become established in their new country. These immigrants had, in the desperate struggle to survive in eastern Europe, perfected marketable skills. Those with skills in the needle trades found immediate employment; others willingly learned new skills. These hard-working immigrants added great variety to American Jewry.

A Growing Tide of Hatred

Ominous voices of hatred could be heard more loudly than ever before in America—the focus of prejudice against the Jew was sharpened. Often old-line American Protestants expressed fear of Jews as well as Catholics. One such voice was that of Thomas E. Watson, a Southern Baptist lawyer, publisher, and layman, and a successful pamphleteer whose anti-Catholic, anti-Jewish hate literature brought him a private fortune. Watson voiced his hatred of the Jews in conjunction with debate concerning the trial of Leo Frank, a northern Jew who was convicted in Atlanta, Georgia, and lynched on the slimmest evidence for the murder of a fourteen-year-old girl. It is hard to believe that the principal testimony against Frank was delivered by the only other suspect in the case. Watson saw Frank not only as a guilty individual but as a member of a debased and hated race: "Every student of Sociology knows that the black man's lust after the white woman is not much fiercer than the lust of the licentious Jew for the Gentile." When the press generally questioned the guilty verdict against Frank, Watson immediately charged that the newspapers were in the hands of Jewish interests and that a Jewish-inspired conspiracy was attempting to dictate to the American people.

An examination of Watson's rantings indicates that he supported the lowest and most unsubstantiated charges made against the Jews. He claimed that ritual murder was a common Jewish practice, and that the Jews and Rome were in league. It is distressing that Watson found a receptive audience for his writings and a sympathetic hearing for his accusations. He polled 1,000,000 votes as a Populist Party candidate in 1896, and in 1920 was elected to the United States Senate.

Another infamous episode in the history of American anti-Semitism is associated with the Ku Klux Klan. Following World War I a wave of disillusionment swept the American people and showed itself in political isolationism. The atmosphere was conducive to nativist organizations. The Klan, originally organized in 1867 as an "invisible Empire of the South," was a white, Protestant, underground resistance movement in opposition to Negroes, carpetbaggers, and anyone promoting reconstruction measures. The original Klan was disbanded, only to be reorganized on Stone Mountain near Atlanta in 1915 by Colonel William J. Simmons, a Protestant preacher and promoter. The Klan, as he envisaged it, would be a "high-class, mystic, social, patriotic" order whose goals were to be the protection of womanhood and the supremacy of white Protestants. In practical terms, this euphemistic jargon meant violence, murder, and the spreading of hatred and fear of Negroes, Catholics, and Jews. Again it is alarming to realize the success of such a group. At first the reorganized Klan was small but membership rose to approximately 5,000,000 in its heyday, from 1924 to 1928. The Klan was short-lived due to its own infamy and estimates are that its membership had dropped to 30,000 by 1930.

All this anti-Catholic and anti-Jewish pressure brought political results. For years immigration laws were the prime target of nativist groups. On May 27, 1924, President Coolidge signed the Johnson-Lodge Bill restricting immigration to 2 per cent for each nationality resident in the United States as of the census of 1890. The anti-Jewish intent and result of this bill is shown by the fact that the annual average immigration of Jews, which in the preceding years had been about 50,000, declined to less than 10,000 after 1925.

Circulating at this time were theories of Jewish inferiority because of race. The theory that received some support from anthropologists was that human life had evolved from several different sources—some superior, others inferior. Usually the Jews were considered descendants of an inferior racial stock. The foolishness of such ideas has long since been proven. Yet in the 1920's many books espoused this theory. A typical American example is Madison Grant's *The Passing of the Great Race.*

The fraudulent book *The Protocols of the Elders of Zion,* published in London in 1905, was speedily republished in Boston. *The Protocols* was for years circulated throughout America and became the textbook of much anti-Semitic thought. One of the most tragic episodes in the history of American anti-Semitism was the stature given *The Protocols* by the hero of American industrialism, Henry Ford. Ford, owner of the *Dearborn Independent,* printed much anti-Semitic propaganda over a seven-year period based on the assumption that there was a Jewish international conspiracy to rule the world. Ford's source of authority was *The Protocols,* which he also published. The basic series of ninety-six articles, which originally appeared in the *Independent* in the 1920's, was later reprinted under the title *The International Jew.*

Finally, largely through the efforts of Arthur Brisbane, editor of the Hearst newspapers, Ford became convinced that there was no basis in fact for the assumption of a Jewish conspiracy and that he was doing a great injustice to an innocent people. Furthermore, Brisbane pointed out, *The Protocols* was an obvious forgery. In a letter to Mr. Louis Marshall, chairman of the American Jewish Committee and a prominent citizen of the State of New York, Ford wrote an apology confessing that he was "deeply mortified that this journal, which is intended to be constructive and not destructive, has been made the medium for resurrecting exploded fictions, for giving currency to the so-called Protocols of the Wise Men of Zion, which has been demonstrated, as I learn, to be gross forgeries, and for contending that the Jews have been engaged in a conspiracy to control the capital and the industries of the world, besides laying at their door many offenses against decency, public order and good morals."

But the vicious seed had been sown, the name of an American industrial leader—a man of great prominence—had given credence to a work which debased and spread fear of the Jews. Years before Hitler, Henry Ford popularized the idea of an international Jew. As was to be expected, *The Protocols* and *The International Jew,* using Henry Ford's name, were published by anti-Semitic organizations in Mexico, South America, and the United States, even after Ford's apology. Both works were also used in the 1930's by the Nazi propaganda machine.

In general the 1920's witnessed a great deal of propagandizing by anti-Semites. In addition to the tons of hate material published by Ford there were organizations devoted to the distribution of malicious anti-Semitic material. Such publishing concerns as The American Standard in New York, The Fellowship Forum in Washington, and The Searchlight in Atlanta berated the Jews. Rumors of ritual murder circulated throughout the country. When Roosevelt introduced the New Deal many Americans contemptuously brushed it off as a "Jew deal."

The Climax: The 1930's

The decade following 1930 saw a frightening increase in group prejudice against the Jews in the United States. At no other time in history has America experienced such anti-Semitic outbursts. To be sure the anti-Semitism of that time was an expression in America of an international phenomenon. Previously anti-Semitism in this country had been largely subtle, but now it became bold and blatant, spurred on by a depression, the initiation of the New Deal, and the influence of rabid anti-Semitism in Nazi Germany. A whole profusion of new groups emerged. One scholar has counted as many as 121 anti-Semitic organizations active in America during this period.

Perhaps the best known was the German-American Bund, or The Friends of New Germany. The Bund, whose membership at its peak in 1938 reached 20,000 to 25,000 people, required in its membership pledges the following statement: "I am of Aryan descent, free of Jewish or colored racial traces." One of the Bund's most spectacular programs was the attempt to inculcate the Nazi philosophy in children. Every effort was made to tighten the grip on all German-American youngsters on the basis that such were destined to carry forward the Nazi ideas and ultimately bring victory to German ideals in this country. Even more spectacular than the youth groups was the Storm Troop auxiliary of the Bund.

The uniform was similar to the German Storm Troopers and all the larger locals had select members in this organization. In the background was the thought that the Storm Troopers might be useful in some period of internal strife. The Bund's major activity however was the spreading of propaganda. Four official Bund newspapers served the nation. Tons of propagandist literature were smuggled into the country from Germany and some literature was published here. A few of these titles are *Positive Christianity, Blood and Race, The New Germany Under Hitler,* and *The Riddle of the Jews' Success.*

While the German-American Bund was made up almost entirely of German-born persons and was both controlled and subsidized by Germany, many other organizations grew out of the American scene—their membership predominantly old American stock. One such organization was the Silvershirts. It came into existence in February, 1933, reaching its greatest membership of 15,000 in the summer of 1934. Organizer William Dudley Pelley, born in Lynn, Massachusetts, in 1885, who dominated this group, let it be known that his paternal forebears were of "purest English stock." Raised in the home of a fundamentalist Methodist itinerant preacher, Pelley seems to have remained religiously frustrated throughout his life. Never able to shake the fundamentalism of his childhood, which failed to satisfy him, Pelley took up spiritualism, which also failed to provide an adequate expression of his desires. Anti-Semitism, on the other hand, seemed to fulfill Pelley as nothing else had been able to do. Here was a channel not only for externalizing his aggression, but also for releasing the bitterness generated by years of frustration. Pelley attempted to lead a nationwide movement of Silvershirted men to drive the Jews and the revolutionaries from power.

The Silvershirts' two chief channels of propaganda were a weekly magazine, *Liberation,* and a weekly newspaper, *The Silver Legion Rangers. Liberation* reached a circulation of around 50,000 in 1933. Although the chief function of the Silvershirts was always the dissemination of anti-Semitic propaganda, the San Diego unit prepared for retaliation by violent action. The membership purchased amunition and arms and trained to resist in the event that Communists attempted to stage a revolution in San Diego on

May Day, 1934. It was their plan to counterattack and beseige City Hall. The Silvershirts were obsessed with the notion that a Jewish-inspired Communist revolt was imminent.

Helping to spread anti-Semitism throughout America during the middle years of the 1930's was a Roman Catholic priest, Father Charles E. Coughlin, organizer of the National Union for Social Justice. Coughlin, born in Hamilton, Ontario, Canada, in 1891, began a career as a radio personality on Station WJR in Detroit in 1936. He proclaimed that the one simple explanation for the country's woes was the fact that communistic Jews were involved in a conspiracy against the United States.

Coughlin's ideology was spread through the popular mediums of radio and newspaper. His programs were heard on a network of forty-seven stations at one point in his career. *Social Justice,* his weekly newspaper, was sold on the newsstands of the nation's cities and its circulation of about 1,000,000 made it the nation's most widely read anti-Semitic periodical. Although it was published in Coughlin's church the paper was unfortunately considered a private enterprise not subject to ecclesiastical control.

Like so many other anti-Semitic propagandists, Coughlin was guilty of outright misquotation and manufacturing authorities. For example, in connection with the 1920 celebration of Lincoln's birthday, Coughlin asserted that the American Civil War was not fought over slavery, but to free the United States from Jewish international bankers. He proceeded to verify this absurd claim by reference to an out-of-print book. On another occasion, Coughlin asserted that two Polish rabbis had admitted the authenticity of *The Protocols of the Elders of Zion.* Investigation revealed that the two rabbis had never existed except in Coughlin's imagination.

It is difficult to ascertain the size of Coughlin's following. Perhaps the best estimate of the size of his radio audience was made by the American Institute of Public Opinion in January, 1939. Of some 3,500,000 listeners, the Institute estimated that two thirds approved his ideas. Undoubtedly the majority of Coughlin's followers were Catholics many of them unaware of the fact that Coughlin's superior, the late Cardinal Mundelein, had stated that Coughlin "is not authorized to speak for the Catholic Church, nor does he represent the doctrine or sentiments of the Church."

While Coughlin's National Union for Social Justice was a predominantly Catholic expression of anti-Semitism many other groups appealed to a fiery type of Protestant fundamentalism and found within it a good climate for anti-Semitism. The Reverend Gerald B. Winrod, publisher of a monthly magazine, *The Defender,* and a newspaper, *The Revealer,* was one such man. In the mid-1930's Winrod became convinced that behind Protestant modernism—which he considered the grossest of evils—and every other evil in the material world there was what he called Jewish bolshevism. Then too there was an organization known as The American Christian Defenders, or The World Alliance Against Jewish Aggressiveness, organized by Colonel E. N. Sanctuary in New York City in 1934. Sanctuary based his anti-Semitism on an alleged personal experience. He claimed that when he was in charge of a railroad division during World War I he saw documents in which Jewish interests supplied $1,000,000 to Lenin and Trotsky in order to finance the Russian Revolution. He could not produce these documents because they had been destroyed, and he was evasive when asked for a precise description.

Unfortunately this drastic rise in anti-Semitism was again reinforced by a national American hero. In a speech in September, 1941, Charles A. Lindbergh charged that the Jews were a great danger to the United States due to their large holdings and influence in the mass media of communication and in government.

The Exoneration: World War II

This tragic phase of American history—a time of blatant anti-Semitic propaganda, much of it with religious overtones—came to an end with World War II. American anti-Semitism was built, not principally upon the charge of deicide, but upon the assumption that Jews were not loyal Americans and that a Jewish conspiracy was attempting to overthrow the country. Thousands of Jewish young men proved the fallaciousness of these charges as they fought and died in the service of their country in the years 1939 to 1945.

Postwar Years

In the years since the last World War America has shown an inability to completely shake off the shackles of anti-Semitism. George Lincoln Rockwell and his handful of followers have threatened to finish what Hitler began, the Ku Klux Klan has attempted to revive itself, anti-Semitic literature is still being distributed in alarming amounts, and such organizations as the John Birch Society have shown an inclination toward anti-Semitic activity. In 1960, during the worldwide swastika epidemic, six hundred synagogues in the United States were desecrated. Subtle anti-Semitism in the form of exclusion from clubs or residential areas is a regrettable fact on the American scene. These factors remind us that anti-Semitic feeling is still present within our culture; and while in the midst of prosperity anti-Semitism may seem to pass from the scene, its potential remains an ever-present threat.

On the other hand, the other side of America's ambivalent response to the Jew must be recognized. There have been opportunities for the free expression of belief in the United States. The Jewish people have found in this country a place where they can worship in freedom; their synagogues have not been padlocked, nor their Talmuds burned. Jews have made a remarkable contribution in all areas of American life. In response the American people have rejected the views of the overt anti-Semites. The Watsons, Pelleys, and Rockwells are not significant names in this nation's history. Despite the incidents of anti-Semitism which have persisted, America has been a land of hope and opportunity for the largest community of Jews in the world. It is not without significance that the words on the base of the Statue of Liberty are those of the Jewish American poet, essayist, and philanthropist Emma Lazarus:

> Give me your tired, your poor,
> Your huddled masses yearning to be free,
> The wretched refuse of your teeming shore
> Send them, the homeless, tempest torn, to me.
> I lift my lamp beside the golden door.

13

Catastrophe Under the Swastika

The history of the Jews abounds in suffering, persecution, and annihilation. But the most dreadful of catastrophes overcame them in our own time—through one man and one people—a man who was obsessed with anti-Semitic superstition and a people who handed over to him all the powers of the state and of a highly developed technology.

Hitler's Philosophy

Adolf Hitler first encountered anti-Semitism during his years in Vienna. He was then little more than a social outcast, who spent his nights in men's shelters and kept his head above water by selling postcards he had painted himself. He bought his first anti-Semitic brochures for a few pennies at a newsstand. The result of his reading was startling. "Wherever I went I now saw Jews, and the more I saw the more distinct they became from other people." And later, "Was there any filth, any indecency in whatever form, especially in the cultural life, in which at least one Jew did not have a part? As soon as one carefully cut into such a growth, one found, like a maggot in the putrefying flesh, a little kike."

Hitler wrote these words in his book, *Mein Kampf*. The awkward and pompous language shows that anti-Semitism had become his "inspiration." All at once he had an extremely simple explanation for everything he disliked in the world, whether it were socialism or capitalism, modern art, pacifism, or parliaments. Everything

129

Hitler hated—and hate was one of the main forces that motivated him—was in his opinion caused by the Jews. No further thought was necessary. At the same time anti-Semitism gave him the feeling, in spite of his low social status, of belonging to an "elite," namely the chosen Aryan race. This raised him far above the "subhuman Jews"—without the slightest effort on his part.

There is no doubt that for Hitler anti-Semitism was not merely just one propaganda tool among many, but represented deep-seated personal delusions. This became abundantly clear after his rise to power.

The Victory of the Swastika

The end of World War I found the German people in a situation that for several reasons was a fertile ground for anti-Semitism. Even during the war the historian Gustav Mayer had watched the growth of anti-Semitism:

The longer the war dragged on, the more frequently I heard that during the seemingly unending trench warfare German soldiers kept themselves apart from their Jewish comrades. From the front this new anti-Semitic wave reached the homeland. Even the most bedraggled Spanish peasant, so said the Frenchman Jean Linguet even before the Revolution, feels less miserable as long as he has a donkey on whose back he can vent his discontent with impunity. The new German anti-Semitism stemmed primarily from the discontented masses' need for a whipping-boy. In place of donkeys it was the Jews.

National self-confidence was deeply undermined by the defeat and the Versailles Treaty, especially its war guilt clause. Chauvinism was revived. The transition to parliamentary democracy demanded greater responsibility from all citizens. Now everyone was to do his part, to participate in self-government, but for many this was an uncomfortable task. It seemed far easier to fight "Judah" than to contribute to the betterment of political conditions.

Hitler shrewdly exploited this state of affairs. His slogan "Germany, awake!" appealed to the injured feelings of national honor; it was much simpler to inveigh with fiery phrases against the

"Versailles dictate" from a speaker's platform than for responsible politicians to discuss it around a conference table. The idea of a dictatorship—"Leader, command, we follow you"—became increasingly popular the more the political parties showed themselves incapable of governing, the more they quarreled over abstract points instead of seeking practical solutions.

When in 1929 the world economic crisis broke out, Hitler reaped the full benefit from the weaknesses of the Weimar Republic. Under the impact of the unemployment of millions, it became clear that the citizens of the Weimar Republic had not enough trust in themselves and their new state to face the crisis with the patience and confidence shown by other democracies. The vote for Hitler jumped from less than 5 per cent to 18.5 per cent, and in 1932 to 37.2 per cent. On the basis of these election victories Hitler was appointed German Chancellor on January 30, 1933.

The role played by anti-Semitic propaganda in his accession to power was unmistakable. The twenty-five–point program of the National Socialist German Workers' Party demanded that the Jews be treated as aliens. Naturally, Jews were not admitted to the meetings of the party. In the streets the storm troopers sang: "When Jewish blood runs from our knives, then everything goes twice as well!" The horrible slogan, "Death to the Jews!" could be seen on every poster next to the swastika (originally an Indo-Germanic sun symbol, it had been misappropriated by the fanatic racists.). This "cross of the gallows" became the symbol of hate, terror, and bloody persecutions.

Doubtless every country contains a number of people who are attracted by brutality and violence. But that such vast masses of voters were not repelled by it remains incomprehensible. True, one has to take into account that German political thought as formed by Bismarck made a distinction between party politicians and statesmen. The first were the talkers, the others the doers. Campaign speeches were generally not taken seriously. Instead, the electorate hoped that, once in office, the politician would miraculously acquire the moderation and wisdom that are part of the responsible statesman. Hence, there were many who thoughtlessly believed that the National Socialists' bark was worse than their bite. This turned out to be a fateful and terrible error.

The Jews Are Outlawed and Isolated

Characteristically, even after Hitler's seizure of power practically no spontaneous anti-Semitic excesses took place. In spite of all the hate-mongering, hardly anyone was prepared to use personal violence. Many Germans continued to buy in Jewish shops and to use Jewish doctors. Hence Hitler had to resort to legal and administrative measures. Since a politically deluded people had entrusted him with total power, there was no opposition, no free press, no judiciary to stop him. Perhaps the Germans would have objected and protested more vigorously if they had clearly recognized the goal of all these measures. But Hitler was shrewd enough to proceed only step by step. Thus the Germans watched passively while their Jewish neighbors were outlawed and generally isolated.

On March 28, 1933, the Nazi leadership ordered a boycott of Jewish stores. The shops were picketed by storm troopers carrying huge signs saying "Don't buy from Jews!" While this campaign affected Jewish trade, it by no means completely drove away the customers.

In April, 1933, a "Law for the Reestablishment of the Professional Civil Service" provided for the discharge of "non-Aryan" officials. This and similar laws clearly demonstrated the utter inanity of the racial doctrine. Since it was impossible to establish the racial characteristics which the regime had so steadfastly maintained existed, the religious denomination of parents or grandparents determined who was a "Racial Jew"! Inversely, the baptismal certificates of all four grandparents were accepted as proof of Aryan descent. If one of these certificates could not be produced, one was classed as "quarter Jewish"; if it was missing for one parent or two grandparents, one was "half Jewish."

The next major assault took place at the 1935 Nuremberg Party Congress, where the "Nuremberg Laws," which turned the Jews into second-class citizens, were proclaimed. These laws prohibited marriage and extramarital relations between Jews and "Citizens of German blood," although the already existing marriages between "Aryans" and "non-Aryans" were not legally invalidated. Soon, however, increasing pressure was exerted on the "Aryan" partner to seek a divorce. After such a divorce, the Jewish partner became the defenseless prey of countless reprisals. Often suicide seemed to be the only way out. The poet Jochen Klepper and the actor Joachim Gottschalk, both married to Jewish women, were so harassed by this law that they and their families finally chose death.

November 9, 1938, and Thereafter

A further number of anti-Semitic laws were issued after November 9, 1938, the date on which Herschel Grynspan, a Polish Jew, killed Ernst von Rath, a German diplomat, in Paris. The synagogues all over Germany were put to the torch by storm troopers—but that was only the beginning. Two hundred and sixty-seven synagogues were gutted; in addition, 815 stores were destroyed, 20,000 Jews arrested, and 36 killed. Joseph Goebbels, the Minister of Propaganda, impudently proclaimed that these acts of arson, which had been personally ordered and supervised by him, were "the spontaneous reaction of the German people." It might be truer to say that these acts of destruction caused spontaneous indignation, which, however did not suffice to stop Hitler.

On the contrary, the party leadership had apparently waited only for a cue to rush its anti-Semitic program into action. The victims of the "Crystal Night," the Jews, not the real culprits, the storm troopers, were ordered to pay a "penalty" of one billion marks. Furthermore, the Jews had to pay the costs of all repairs. Shortly thereafter an order for the "elimination of the Jews from German economic life" was issued. Jews were no longer allowed to own shops, follow a trade, or occupy leading positions in any business. The Minister of Education ordered the dismissal of all Jewish students from German schools. In many localities a so-called "Jew Ban" was announced—that is, Jews were forbidden to set foot in certain districts and to patronize movies, museums, and theaters.

At that time many Jewish families decided to emigrate—if they could possibly manage to do so. They had to sell their homes and furniture for a song, but at least they avoided the far worse fate that, after the outbreak of war, awaited those who either had been unable to leave or had insisted on staying in their homeland despite all threats (later, many of these patriots had to pay with their lives for their love of Germany).

Today, the emigrants' fate appears to us a deliverance from a terrible end in Auschwitz or Maidanek. But their fate also almost invariably had its tragic aspects. Stefan Zweig, himself a refugee, wrote this in his reminiscences:

Week after week, month after month, more refugees arrived, and every week they were poorer and more distraught than those who had come before them. Those who came first, who had promptly left Germany or Austria, had still been able to salvage their clothes, their baggage, their household goods and some of them even a little money. But the longer someone had put his trust in Germany, the more difficult it had been for him to tear himself away from his beloved homeland, the harder he had been chastised. . . . They stood at the frontiers, they begged at the consulates and almost always in vain, for what country wanted beggars, people stripped of all they had? I shall never forget the sight that once met my eyes in a London travel agency; it was crammed full with refugees, almost all of them Jews, and all of them wanted to go somewhere. No matter to which country, to the ice of the North Pole or to the hot sands of the Sahara. They had to move on, for their residence permits had expired, they had to push on, with wife and child to strange lands, among people speaking a foreign language, among people who did not know them and did not want them. There I met a formerly very rich Viennese industrialist, one of our most discriminating art collectors; at first I did not recognize him, he had become so gray, so old, so tired. Feebly he grasped the desk with both hands. I asked him where he wanted to go. "I don't know," he said. "Who asks us today what we want? We go where we are still allowed to go. Somebody has told me that one can perhaps get a visa for Haiti or Santo Domingo." My heart stopped; here was an old, deadly tired man with children and grandchildren, trembling with hope at the prospect of going to a country he had hardly heard of, to end up begging his way from place to place, to go on forever being an alien and utterly useless! . . . And so they jostled each other, former university professors, bank directors, businessmen, musicians, everyone prepared to drag the miserable fragments of his existence across land and sea, to do and suffer whatever was necessary, only to get away from Europe, away, away!

Escape was followed by homelessness and homesickness, and many of the refugees ended as suicides; Stefan Zweig himself put an end to his life in Brazil, Kurt Tucholsky in Sweden, Ernst Toller in New York, Walter Benjamin at the French-Spanish frontier in order to escape the approaching German troops.

The war favored the use of refined chicaneries, as most people were preoccupied with their own worries. From July, 1940, on, in many places Jews were allowed to shop only during certain hours. Later they could buy only in a few stores set aside for them. In September, 1941, a decree was issued requiring Jews above the age of six to wear in public "a palm-sized, yellow six-cornered star with the word 'Jew' in black on the left side of their chest." The choice of the Star of David for this mark of infamy was particularly vile.

This was followed in October, 1941, by the forced-labor decree. The Jews had already been forced, as far as was feasible, to work in factories. Now they were no longer covered by the minimum wage law nor even protected by the labor laws! The degree to which legislation was abused for the most petty humiliations was disgraceful. During the year 1942 the legal gazettes abounded in decrees of the following kind: The homes of Jews must be marked with a Star of David; Jews are no longer allowed to keep pets; Jews are not allowed to own electric appliances, record players, records, typewriters, bicycles, radios; Jews are not allowed to use public shelters; and so on.

The Return of the Ghetto

But since November, 1941, this policy of refined torments had been overshadowed by a much more terrible threat.

Hitler's victories had not only made him master over life and death of the German Jews, but exposed 3,300,000 Jews in Poland, 300,000 in France, 150,000 in Holland, and later 2,100,000 in the Russian-occupied territories to his frenzy of annihilation. In some of these countries their Christian fellow citizens protected the Jews as well as they could. When the decree forcing the Jews to wear a yellow Star of David was introduced in France, there were demonstrations of friendship: on the streets the branded Jews were greeted with open cordiality and non-Jews sported yellow flowers or paper Stars of David in their lapels. In Denmark King Christian announced in a message to the people that all Danes were equally close to his heart, that he would be the first one, therefore, to wear the Star of David, and that he expected all his loyal subjects to follow suit. As a result, the Nazis had to withdraw this anti-Jewish decree in Denmark. Later the Danes managed to save a considerable number of their Jewish fellow citizens by ferrying them in fishing vessels to Sweden. In Holland many Jews succeeded in "going underground." Anne Frank's diary pays tribute to the bravery of the Dutch protectors.

In Poland and Russia, however, the situation was different. There most Jews still lived in separate settlements and in many instances were distinguishable by their language and clothing. They could not just blend into the population; moreover, many Poles displayed anti-Semitic tendencies. Hence the SS conceived the idea of creating ghettos there like those of the Middle Ages. The Jews were herded into designated sections of Lublin, Cracow, Warsaw, and Lodz; the entire district was surrounded with fences and marked with signs: "No Admittance, Jewish Sector." Presently, famine and epidemics of every kind ran rampant in these ghettos, and, as no countermeasures were taken, they spread like wildfire. On the pattern of these Polish ghettos an entire ghetto city was established in 1941 in Terezin in Bohemia. It was to serve as a concentration camp for Jews from Germany. In November, 1941, the decree for "Deportation of the Jews" was issued, according to which "Jews not working in enterprises essential for the national economy are to be deported during the next few months to a town in the Eastern Territories. Their property is to be confiscated for the benefit of the German state. Each Jew is permitted to keep 100 marks and 110 pounds of baggage."

In Germany, the rumor was spread that conditions in Terezin were quite "humane": the Jews were permitted cultural autonomy—permitted to put on plays and concerts. This fairy tale only served to lull people's conscience. In reality, this camp, like all others, was an efficiently organized hell in which the inmates, inhumanly herded together, were first crushed emotionally and mentally before they succumbed to hunger. Men who belonged to the Jewish leadership—rabbis, teachers, professors, famous musicians—lived crowded together like cattle. Food was so scarce that a cold potato was prized as a precious gift.

As it worked out, however, Terezin was only a transit station on the way to the extermination camps, which were then being established for the "final solution of the Jewish problem."

The "Final Solution of the Jewish Problem"

On July 31, 1941, Reich Marshal Hermann Goering had ordered the chief of the Security Police, Heydrich, to submit a master plan for carrying out the "final solution of the Jewish problem." The SS was at that time considering shipping all Jews to the island of Madagascar. But such a plan was obviously unfeasible, and thus Hitler and Himmler came to the conclusion that the Jews had to be "exterminated." The first step was to evacuate them to the East. What was to happen to them there is recorded in a document called the "Wannsee Memorandum," after the place in which the fatal meeting took place.

In the course of the final solution, the Jews, suitably supervised, are to be used for forced labor in the East. In large work columns, the sexes separated, the able-bodied Jews are to be used in road-building on the way to these territories. Undoubtedly natural attrition will greatly reduce their numbers. The remnant, doubtless the hardiest among them, will receive *special treatment,* since, representing a natural selection, they would in case of release be a germ-cell of Jewish reconstruction. . . . In the course of implementation of the final solution, Europe will be combed through from West to East. . . .

In the veiled bureaucratic language of the SS, in the language of barbarians, "special treatment," was a euphemism for "mass murder."

The initial choice for this "special treatment" was mass shooting. The Jews were dragged out of their ghettos, taken to remote places, and forced to dig pits. Next, all of them—men, women, and children—had to undress completely and put their clothes and shoes in a neat pile. Finally, five to ten people at a time had to step to the edge of the pit, to be mowed down with tommy guns. When the mass graves had filled with five hundred to a thousand corpses, they were covered with lime and earth. Himmler once witnessed this method of killing and felt sufficiently nauseated to order a "more humane" method—poison gas—to be used. The gas was piped either into railroad boxcars or into specially constructed chambers disguised as shower rooms.

Installations for this form of mass killing were set up in the extermination camps of Auschwitz, Maidanek, and Treblinka. Gigantic crematoria were built, in which the corpses were burned day and night. As the crowning irony of this fiendish system, the Jews themselves were ordered to service the entire apparatus of slaughter. They had to remove the heaps of corpses from the gas chambers and to tend the crematoria. Their only hope during this terrible work was that perhaps they themselves might thus escape death.

When word spread among the Jews still at liberty of what awaited them at the end of the "deportations," those to whom a helping hand was extended tried to go underground and live "illegally." Such help was offered in Germany, but not enough by far.

For the vast majority, who found no refuge, a martyrdom was mapped out, with always the same way stations: First came labor in enterprises "essential to the war effort," to the point of utter exhaustion, each day filled with the fear that relatives unfit for work might have received the order to be deported East. One day it came for everyone—inescapably. During the last hours many chose death at their own hand. At the collection points all were stripped of the carefully packed vestiges of their belongings. Then came the many days of transport in overcrowded cattle cars. At arrival in the extermination camps the transports were conducted to "selection points," men and women were separated, parents and children torn apart. "At first I was still with my husband," reported Grete Salus, who survived this hell. "We talked and acted mechanically; we simply wanted to cling to something real, something familiar. My girl friend was distributing chocolate. My husband took a piece and said, 'I'll be back in a minute, I'll just run back to the freight car to bring some chocolate to my sick friend.' Those were the last words I heard from him, the last time I saw him. A life, such a rich life had been tossed away. . . . Because he ran back [there], he was destroyed together with the sick. Not even a kiss, not even a hand clasp. . . ."

The sick and the aged, the infirm and the children were ordered to the left at these "selections," death their certain fate. The others, those still able to work, were sent into the barracks. They became slave laborers, subsisting on the most wretched food, until they died of epidemics or hunger or one day were selected for extermination themselves. "A woman in our transport," Grete Salus continued, "the mother of a 12-year old boy and a 14-year old daughter, had heard that children under 16 were being gassed. She had such a pitiful face—such a begging, imploring look that one had to bite one's lips until they bled in order not to burst into tears. 'Do you think it's true?' she asked everyone; we said no, of course; we didn't believe it ourselves. To murder children, that is unthinkable; perhaps the old or the sick people, but children. . . . There was another mother—she had a 15-year old boy—the same expression in her face, and I can still hear her, a helpless little cough, not even tears. None of us cried; we were petrified with terror, and although we were not sure we could not believe what we had heard. . . ." But the unbelievable was true; the stench of the crematoria hovered like a cloud over the camps. The threat of death was ever present.

Nor was this all. In these camps the SS guards conducted roll calls lasting many hours, during which the emaciated and tattered prisoners had to stand in rain, snow, sun, and wind until all inmates had been counted. Woe to any one of these doomed creatures if he dared die unobserved in a barrack on a heap of rags! If one were missing, the counting began all over again, and twenty-four or forty-eight hours might pass before the prisoners were allowed to leave their places. Those who dropped to the ground were kicked and beaten.

A special characteristic was lent this lust for murder by the fact that every death was registered with bureaucratic precision and an "SS Economic and Administrative Office" established for the express purpose of collecting and "processing" by the boxes and tons all the wretched possessions of the victims: their clothing, glasses, dentures, gold teeth, even the women's hair. Human beings were not simply exterminated as if they were vermin; they were also treated as merchandise and exploited as "sources of raw material" for the war effort.

"Like Sheep Led to Slaughter . . ."

The number of those who fell victim to this insane anti-Semitic carnage is incredibly large, so large that the mind refuses to accept it, that the heart is unable to comprehend the suffering this figure encompasses. Of 8,300,000 Jews living in 1939 in all the territories later ravaged by the murdering hosts of the SS, 5,978,000 were missing in 1945. They had been murdered according to plan: by means of hunger, epidemic, machine guns, gas. Utterly defenseless, they had been herded together, from Holland and France, from Yugoslavia and Greece, from Germany and Austria; 2,800,000 of them came from Polish towns and villages. What de we know of them? Their fears, their cries of anguish, their terror in the face of death have all been muffled. But out of the silence of millions a single voice reaches out to us, the voice of a child, a twelve-year-old boy, who in stumbling phrases committed to a few notebooks his fears, his bewilderment, his tremendous suffering. Long after little David Rubinowicz went to his death in Treblinka, a neighbor found his record and safeguarded it.

November 1, 1941

Today notices were put up in Kielce that everyone who leaves or enters the "Jewish Quarter" will be punished by death. Until now, one could enter and leave at will. This order has made me very sad—not only me, but every Jew who has heard it.

December 12, 1941

Yesterday afternoon I went to Bodzentyn because I am making plugs. I spent the night there. Early this morning, the police came. As they drove along the highway they met a Jew who was leaving the town. They shot him without any reason, and as they drove on they shot a Jewish woman too, again without any reason. Thus two victims were killed without any reason. As I walked home I was very much afraid I might meet them; but I didn't meet anyone. . . .

January 12, 1942

First thing this morning I went out to shovel snow. When I went inside to warm myself, the deputy sheriff came and said that he had read the notice at the sheriff's office that the [all] Jews will be evacuated; that they may not take anything with them except the clothes they are wearing. We were so frightened by this news that we didn't know what was happening to us. . . .

April 10, 1942

A peasant from Kranjo came and told us that they had shot the daughter of our former neighbor because she was on the street after 7 o'clock. I don't want to believe it, but everything is possible. This girl is like a flower; that she should be shot—that is really the end of the world. Why must it be that there can't be a single quiet day? . . . Our nerves are already quite worn out. Whenever I hear of some tragedy my eyes protrude from their sockets, my head hurts, and I feel as tired as if I had worked hard all day long. Not only I, everyone. Was it not enough that in the other war the cossacks shot papa's father and he had to watch it; then he had enough, he was 11 years old. When he sees a German now he wants to crawl into a hole, he feels so crushed.

April 18, 1942

Today the weather is beautiful, it hasn't been like this for a long time. If only we had freedom, then everything would be all right. But as things are, one can't even go into the town. Now we are caught like dogs on a chain.

May 6, 1942

A terrible day! . . . All our possessions were taken away; now we have to beg for a piece of bread. Anciel came right away and said that they have caught papa and our cousin too. Only then did I begin to cry. They have taken papa, everything we had they took too. How I long for papa now. Mama went to the Jewish Council to ask them to have papa released. After all, he is sick and cannot live without medication, and now he is supposed to go to a work camp. That's terrible. After it had become a bit quieter, two cars passed; one had a platform in the rear. I sobbed loudly as they came nearer and cried: "Papa, where are you? I want to see you!" I saw him on the last car, crying; I looked at him until the car disappeared behind a curve, and only then I cried loudly and felt how much I loved him. . . .

The Defenseless Resist

The question is asked—and particularly by the younger generation in Israel—How was it possible for the SS to carry out its killings without encountering resistance? Joseph Roth was probably right when in 1927 he wrote that Jews in the countries to the East still had "the historical feeling, fed by experience, that the Jews are always the first victims of the blood baths arranged by world history." This new disaster was like the persecutions and pogroms their fathers and forefathers had had to endure. Yet the method was so monstrous in scope that no one could really believe it possible. They willingly let themselves be deceived by SS men, who took great care to speak only of "resettlement." When the truth finally did filter through, horror paralyzed action. But once the shock wore off, resistance began. It was carried out under the most difficult of circumstances, and the number of those who could be torn from the fiery mouth of the Moloch was small in comparison with the number of those who became his victims. But the selflessness of those who did resist, coupled with their cunning and courage, which made resistance possible, will forever be remembered.

The most significant assistance came from the agents of the Mossad, an organization of daredevil Palestinian Jews who had taken it upon themselves to save as many Jews as possible by any conceivable means and to bring them to Palestine, be it legally or illegally. They established secret resistance cells, procured money and passports, chartered ships, and, whenever necessary, negotiated with the devil himself.

The Mossad agents worked hand in hand with the Jewish resistance fighters. Hungary was occupied by German troops only in March, 1944. Until that time Jews could move about in comparative freedom and a Jewish underground movement came into being which successfully smuggled Jews out of the ghettos and extermination camps under the most hazardous circumstances. Often the Nazi henchmen could be bribed, and lives were bartered for money. The henchmen were aware of the attitude of their superiors. When the SS entered Budapest, the notorious Adolf Eichmann summoned the leader of the Jewish resistance, Joel Brand, in order to propose a deal: "I am prepared to sell you a million Jews. I won't sell you all the Jews. You just can't raise that much money and goods. But one million, that is possible. Goods for blood—blood for goods. Go, collect this million in all countries where there are still Jews left." A few days later Eichmann made his offer more specific: "I offer you a fair deal: you deliver one truck for one hundred Jews. That isn't much is it? Altogether, that comes to ten thousand trucks. The trucks must be brand new and be delivered with trailers." Brand was not very hopeful about ever being able to put his hands on such essential war matériel. But just the same, he took a plane to Constantinople in order to meet with everyone who might help save the last remnant of East European Jewry from destruction. In vain. The offer seemed too improbable, too incredible. In Aleppo, Brand was imprisoned by the British Intelligence Service . . . and the gas chambers and crematoria in Auschwitz continued to do their work.

Within the confines of the Warsaw ghetto, into which at one time 500,000 people had been crowded, the last survivors decided to resist to the end. In July, 1942, the SS began to ship 5,000 Jews a day to the extermination camps of Treblinka and Belzec. First the women and children were "combed out," to use the SS jargon. The children had been indispensable to the ghetto as smugglers, for they were able to slip undetected past the checkpoints or through the sewers in order to barter or beg for food. Thus these little heroes helped their families survive. When the number of children without parents began to increase steadily because of the influx from the country, a ghetto self-help organization established orphanages and children's homes to care for them. The teachers and aids in these homes pledged themselves to remain with their charges to the very end. Thus Janusz Korczak, an eminent neurologist and pedagogue, who founded and headed a Jewish orphanage in Warsaw, accompanied the children entrusted to him to their death, though he could have saved himself.

Toward the end of 1942, 400,000 Jews had been evacuated from Warsaw and shipped to the extermination camps. About 35,000 remained behind; they were still needed as workers for the armament workshops located in the ghetto. In January, 1943, the Jewish resistance organization appealed to them to take up arms:

We too were given the gift of life. We have a right to it. But we must stand up and fight for it. . . . Awake, Jews, fight for your lives! Let every mother become a lioness in the defense of her young. No father should be made to witness the death of his child! Down with cowardice and doubt! Make the enemy pay with his blood for every Jewish life! Make every house a fortress! . . . Only those who fight for their lives have the chance to survive!

From then on, subterranean bunkers were built feverishly every night. The Polish underground smuggled weapons into the ghetto. Primitive hand grenades and Molotov cocktails for use against tanks were manufactured secretly in the workshops. When on April 18, 1943, troops of the Armed SS marched into the ghetto in order to "resettle" the rest of the Jewish population, they met with stubborn resistance and were forced to retreat again and again. The Jewish fighters, among them women and girls, converted every doorpost of the ghetto into a fortress and defended themselves in this unequal struggle, with the courage of the doomed. "Perhaps we'll all die in this battle, but surrender we will not" claimed the fighters in their message to the Polish population.

It took more than five weeks to force the rebellious ghetto into submission. Most of its inhabitants died in this life-and-death struggle. When the end came, they had to jump out of the burning buildings or perish in the flames. In the bunkers many committed suicide. Only a few managed to escape the murderers; they have told us the story of this heroic uprising in which the spirit of Judah Maccabee, Simon Bar-Kochba, and Rabbi Akiba came to life once again.

On the German side, the leader of the battle of the Warsaw ghetto, SS General Stroop, presented Hitler with a handsomely bound volume of photographs of the horrors his troops had inflicted, and entitled it "The Jewish Quarter in Warsaw has ceased to exist!"

14

A New Beginning

On April 30, 1945, Hitler killed himself, ending a guilt-laden life wrecked by his fanaticism. Thus he put himself beyond the jurisdiction of mortal judges. The German people has had over twenty years to settle its accounts with this "leader into the void" and to develop new principles for the life of their nation. The touchstone for a change of heart and a return to respect for man, to justice, and to humanity is the eradication of anti-Semitism. Those who still harbor this old hatred have hearts of stone and can lead men only into the desert of death. The Jewish prayers for the Day of Atonement point to hate without reason as one of life's sins and harshest afflictions. The philosopher Hermann Cohen said that "whoever indulges in hatred misuses his heart, whose task it is to love." He added, "All hatred is baseless, vain and futile. We have neither reason nor the right to hate human beings. The greatest of mankind's sufferings is caused by the vain hatred of men, the tragic characteristic of world history."

On May 14, 1948, the State of Israel was proclaimed in Palestine. Decades of hard work had wrested fertile soil from the desert, step by step. The "sons of peddlers and the grandsons of prophets," as Chaim Weizmann, the first President of the new state, once said, had become farmers who doggedly battled the barren earth. The new state had hardly been born when they had to defend it, gun in hand. But the Jews of Israel passed this trial by fire. The Star of David, blue on white ground, was hoisted as the banner of an ancient people over the young state. Thus the land that God had promised Abraham was returned to the Jewish people as its home. Tens of thousands of refugees, driven from all countries of Europe, fleeing for their very lives, could now, in their own land, under their own laws, hold up their heads again and breath freely. On July 5,

1950, the "Law of Return" was passed, granting Jews from all over the world the right to settle in Israel.

Theodor Herzl had said, "Once the Jews again have a state of their own, the Jewish question too will be solved." Doubtless, the existence of the State of Israel is of the greatest importance to Jews the world over. Whether a Jew chooses to make use of his right of return is his personal decision and his alone. The right of Jews to live in peace elsewhere in the world is primarily a matter for Christian conscience. The Russian philosopher of religion Solovyev wrote as early as 1884 that in the course of history the Christians have yet to learn to treat the Jews according to Christian teachings. "In dealing with them we have constantly violated the dictates of Christianity and are still doing so." Hence the time has finally come for those who maintain they are Christians—and who, according to a saying of their Lord, should be the salt of the earth—to fulfill toward the Jews the commandment of love, which first appears in the Old Testament and which should truly unite the peoples of the Old and the New Covenant.

But those who are not professing Christians should reflect that in our day the basic principles of state and society are liberty, equality, and fraternity. The Jews living among us were first granted liberty: they were released from the prison of the ghetto. Gradually they were granted equality: equal opportunities in professional life, equal rights in the state. But we still owe fraternity, not only to them, but also to other oppressed minorities. If the races, nations, and religions of the world fail to learn how to live together as brothers should, they stand to lose their own liberty as well as their human dignity.

We must make a new beginning. But this beginning cannot be marked by either forgiving or forgetting.

Forgiveness rests with the judge. Ours can only be boundless, unquenchable mourning. Only if our mourning is truly inextinguishable can it be an honest response to the horror of what has happened. We must never forget what has been done on German soil by German hands to the Jews; this is the victims' stern bequest to the survivors.

With these words of the poet Margarete Susman in mind, let us all probe our own hearts.

15

Toward Authentic Relationship*

Recent Statements of Protestant Bodies

Contacts between Jews and Christians, both Protestant and Catholic, have increased greatly in recent years. Since the war and the racial holocaust of the Nazi regime many Christian denominations have produced statements of repentance and regret over the sin of anti-Semitism and have resolved to attempt to rid Christianity of it. For example, the American Baptist Convention meeting in Philadelphia in May, 1962, registered "opposition to anti-Semitism which persistently raises its ugly head, creating tensions, hatred and violence." This Convention called Baptist people to "strive for the elimination of all prejudice and discrimination against the Jewish people in every walk of life, and to work for a closer relationship between our Christian and Jewish groups." The Episcopal Church at its sixty-first Triennial Convention in St. Louis in 1964 declared that "the charge of deicide against the Jews is a tragic misunderstanding of the inner significance of the crucifixion. To be sure Jesus was crucified by some Roman soldiers at the instigation of some Jews. But this cannot be construed as imputing corporate guilt to every Jew in Jesus' day—much less the Jewish people in subsequent generations."

At the Amsterdam meeting of the World Council of Churches in 1948 many Protestant denominations joined in acknowledging the Christian responsibility for the fate of European Jews.

* This chapter is by Robert H. Roberts and is new in this translation.— EDITOR.

No people in His one world suffered more bitterly from the disorder of man than the Jewish people. We cannot forget that we meet in a land [Holland] from which 110,000 Jews were taken to be murdered; nor can we forget that we meet only five years after the extermination of six million Jews. . . . We must acknowledge, in all humility, that too often we have failed to manifest Christian love toward our Jewish neighbours. . . . We have failed to fight with all our strength the age-old disorder of man which anti-Semitism represents. The Churches in the past have helped to foster an image of the Jews as the sole enemies of Christ which has contributed to anti-Semitism in the secular world. . . .

The members of the World Council challenged the churches to mount an attack upon all forms of anti-Semitism. Their resolution stated:

We call upon all the Churches we represent to denounce anti-Semitism, no matter what its origin, as absolutely irreconcilable with the profession and practice of the Christian faith. Anti-Semitism is a sin against God and man. . . .

The Catholic Voice

The most famous Christian document dealing with Christian-Jewish relations and the evil of anti-Semitism was issued at the Roman Catholic Ecumenical Council, which met from 1962 to 1965. The Council's concern with a fraternal encounter with the Jews was a response to Pope John XXIII's famous words in which he embraced the Jewish people: "I am Joseph your brother" (Genesis 45:4). Indeed the hopes stirred up within the Jewish community about Vatican II were the result of admiration and respect for Pope John. The Jewish community responded to this pope as it had to no other pope in history. Before ascending to the papacy Pope John was a papal legate in the Near East, where during World War II he made visas available to many Jews, providing them the possibility of refuge and safety. One of Pope John's first acts as head of the church was to remove from the Good Friday liturgy the statement, "Let us pray for the perfidious Jew." An example of the Pope's appeal to the Jews may be seen in his statement in *Pacem in Terris,* "Every human being has the right to honor God according to the dictates of an upright conscience." It is not surprising that there were prayers of mourning in many of the world's synagogues at his passing.

In January, 1962, Cardinal Bea, another Roman Catholic leader greatly respected in the Jewish community, in anticipation of the Vatican Council expressed the belief that the "greatest challenge to our generation is the problem of group antagonism and it is the primordial duty of all groups of mankind to unite for the purposes of overcoming hatreds of the past." Cardinal Bea then met with the French-Jewish scholar Jules Isaac and with Rabbi Abraham Heschel of the United States. Following these discussions the Cardinal outlined what he felt should be the major points in a document concerning the church's relationship to the Jews. Among them were the church's inseparable bond with Judaism; the clear statement by the Council of Trent that the death of Jesus was the responsibility of all mankind; the fact that Christ's mother, the apostles, and the early Christians were all of the seed of Abraham; and the conviction that the Catholic church should never teach a contrary doctrine, but should at all costs promote understanding of the Jews.

Many conservative voices were raised in opposition to such a forthright statement. Even though Cardinal Bea had gone out of his way to insist that the statement in no way referred to the Arab-Israeli conflict, many bishops, particularly those in the Near East, argued that such a statement would be misinterpreted as political backing of the State of Israel. Others felt that ecumenism must be restricted to Christians only. For a time in 1963 rumors spread that there would be no statement at all. Fortunately such rumors proved unfounded.

In 1965, in its "Declaration on the Relationship of the Church to Non-Christian Religions," Vatican II issued an historic statement on the Jews. The statement begins with a recognition of the spiritual bond which links the "people of the New Covenant with Abraham's stock" and continues:

> The Church, therefore, cannot forget that she received the revelation of the Old Testament through the people with whom God in His inexpressible mercy deigned to establish the Ancient Covenant.

The statement goes on to insist that while "Jerusalem did not recognize the time of her visitation," nonetheless "the Jews still remain most dear to God because of their fathers." Since the spiritual patrimony is so great, the Church seeks to foster mutual understanding, respect, and fraternal dialogue with the Jews.

Concerning deicide, Vatican II said:

True, authorities of the Jews and those who followed their lead pressed for the death of Christ . . . still, what happened in His passion cannot be blamed upon all the Jews then living, without distinction, nor upon the Jews of today.

In the church's catechetical or preaching ministry the Jews are not to be presented as "rejected or accursed by God."

The Church repudiates all persecutions against any man. Moreover, mindful of her common patrimony with the Jews, and motivated by the gospel's spiritual love and by no political considerations, she deplores the hatred, persecutions, and displays of anti-Semitism directed against the Jews at any time and from any source.

Some Jews, Protestants, and Catholics were disappointed in the text of this document. They felt it was weak in comparison with earlier proposals. They were disappointed that in view of the close historical relationship between Christianity and Judaism such a statement should be included in a declaration on the relation of the church to non-Christian religions. In the light of the church's historical failure in its relationship to the Jews, many were disappointed that the statement lacked any expression of repentance for the evils the church had committed.

However, it is important to notice the positive construction of this statement. In the first place the Jewish roots of Christianity are recognized and the church is reminded that she received the revelation of the Jewish Bible through the Jews. In the second place the charge of deicide is denied as is the claim that the Children of Israel are accursed or rejected. The statement also asserts forthrightly that anti-Semitism is a sin. In addition, the church is to be sensitive in order to avoid unintentional anti-Semitic statements in its preaching and teaching ministries. Hence this historic "Statement on the Jews" must not be underestimated as a great proclamation of Jewish-Christian relationships. Interpreted in the light of the many statements of repentance for past Christian actions issued by many Catholics, it may be seen as both welcome and helpful.

This document has been taken by the Catholic bishops of the United States as an opportunity to forge ahead toward the development of better understanding between Christians and Jews. On March 16, 1967, the Commission for Catholic-Jewish Relations of the National Council of Catholic Bishops issued an enlightened text entitled "Guidelines for Catholic-Jewish Relations." These guidelines are of such great importance, in that they cover so many of the important issues in Jewish-Christian relations, that they deserve study by Protestants.

This statement lays down general principles the church should adopt in its relationship with the Jews. First, it recommends that each diocese in which both Jews and Catholics live establish a commission or secretariat assigned to Catholic-Jewish affairs. Second, Catholics are urged to take the initiative in fostering Catholic-Jewish relations. Third, the general aim of Catholic-Jewish dialogue is spelled out: to increase the "understanding both of Judaism and the Catholic faith, eliminate sources of tension and misunderstanding, initiate dialogues or conversations on different levels, multiply intergroup meetings between Catholics and Jews, and promote cooperative social action." Fourth, it is to be clearly understood that proselytizing is to be avoided and the meetings characterized by a genuine respect for the person and freedom of the participants. Such meetings should be structured carefully with the aid of persons experienced in structural, doctrinal, and interpersonal skills. Finally, "Prayer in common with the Jews should, whenever it is feasible, be encouraged, especially in matters of common concern, such as peace and the welfare of the community." Such prayers should be acceptable to both Jew and Christian.

The bishops call for such dialogues on all possible levels. Not only are the clergy to be involved through the pastoral offices of teaching and preaching but laymen also are to participate in Catholic-Jewish projects of understanding and action. Catholic scholars, in conjunction with Jewish scholars, must probe in depth the sociological, psychological, theological, biblical, and historical dimensions of specific problems.

Obviously certain themes will emerge as central in Catholic-Jewish dialogue. The Commission for Catholic-Jewish Relations calls for a careful examination of such themes. For instance, efforts should be made to grasp the common heritage possessed by Jew and Christian. A frank and honest treatment of Christian anti-Semitism along with a repudiation of such attitudes is called for. The Commission asks for a study of the life of Jesus in terms of first-century Jewish life. Christians engaged in dialogue are to repudiate the historically inaccurate concept that the Judaism of Jesus' time was a decadent hyper-legalistic religion. Also the crucifixion must be presented in such a way as not to implicate all the Jews of the first century or the Jews of the twentieth century in any form of collective guilt for the death of Jesus. A careful interpretation of the term *the Jews* as it is used in the New Testament is necessary. Finally, the bishops call for a greater awareness by Christians of the post-Christian history of Judaism and a recognition of what Paul alluded to as "the permanent election of Israel" (Romans 9:29).

The Lag of Lay Opinion Behind
Official Pronouncements

This statement coming from the American Catholic church is a most significant document in Jewish-Christian relations and points the way to a new era of understanding among the Catholic, Protestant, and Jewish communities. Unfortunately, such official pronouncements are often far in advance of common practice. This lag is made evident in many ways. An example is the response of the news media to recent church pronouncements concerning the Jews. The impression given by the press is that the church is in some way absolving the Jews for a crime. On the contrary, the Jews were not guilty of the crucifixion of Jesus and the church in its pronouncements has been trying to adjust its own thought so as to accurately express its theology and to relate to the Jews in a manner more consistent with Christian teaching.

"The Jews" in the New Testament

In so doing the church must take into account the unquestionable fact that the term *the Jews* in the New Testament requires careful interpretation. A classic example is the Gospel According to St. John. Here the term *Jews* refers broadly to the opposition to Jesus and his party. The term thus becomes a literary device which allows the author to set up opposition to Jesus and then to show the obvious superiority of Jesus over that opposition. For example, the author of John's Gospel commonly shows Jesus making a statement, which is misinterpreted by "the Jews" and then correctly interpreted either by Jesus himself or by the author. Therefore, as it appears in this Gospel, *the Jews* is simply a literary foil, lacking precise meaning. It does not refer to all the Jewish people of Jesus' day, nor even to all the Jews with whom Jesus came in contact. Indeed some of the heroes of John's Gospel are Jews: the apostles, Mary, Nicodemus, Martha, Lazarus, and even Jesus himself. When one encounters the derisive use of the term *the Jews* in this Gospel one should remember that John quotes Jesus as saying, "Salvation is of the Jews."

Actually the terminology referring to the various Jewish groups in the New Testament is confusing. For instance, St. Luke, like Matthew and John, regards Pharisaism as a degenerate form of religious legalism and sees the Pharisees as major opponents of Jesus. As we have seen, this is an interpretation of Pharisaism which the history of Judaism does not support. To this day, the Law, which Christians characterize as a burden, has hallowed every aspect of Jewish life. Yet in the Book of the Acts, which is really a continuation of the Gospel of Luke, the chief Jewish opposition to the Church comes from the Sadducean Temple authorities in Jerusalem and from the Jews of certain synagogues of the diaspora. In the early part of the Acts the Pharisees are considered neutral or even favorably inclined toward Jesus. The Pharisees in the twenty-third chapter of the Acts attempt to acquit Paul because of his belief in the resurrection from the dead; in the fifth chapter Gamaliel, a Pharisee, is presented as a godly man of great discretion.

From this cursory survey it is evident that terms referring to the

Jews or to sects of Judaism in the New Testament should not be readily identified with entire movements but should be interpreted in terms of the specific context in which they are found.

Clearing Away the Cobwebs in Our Thinking About Deicide

If then it is necessary to interpret New Testament passages referring to the Jews with great care, what can be said of the two major theological accusations which have been leveled at the Jews?—the first, that Jews are guilty of deicide—the murder of Christ—and the second, that the dispersion of the Jews is a visible sign of God's judgment upon them for their rejection of Christ.

The crucifixion of Jesus, which is the central event of the gospel stories, requires major attention. It can be stated categorically that the concept that the Jews are solely guilty of the crucifixion of Jesus is neither historically nor theologically valid. This accusation is a pernicious distortion of the facts.

Deicide is a term which many Christians prefer not to use. Its meaning, the murder of God, refers to the Christian belief that Jesus was the Son of God. Hence to kill Jesus is to kill God, according to such thinking.

The interpretation of the crucifixion is complicated by the fact that the Gospel writers consciously or unconsciously reflect the attitudes of the later struggle between church and synagogue in their writings. Naturally Christians were wanting to make their way in the Roman Empire and to establish the veracity of the new religion. And they were competing with the Jews for converts. It would be well to remember the words of John Knox when reading the New Testament accounts of the crucifixion: "No one can study the Gospel narratives of the Passion without recognizing this tendency to exonerate the Romans and to blame the Jews." This is particularly true in Matthew's Gospel, which strangely enough seems to have been written primarily for the Jews. Here Pilate (who was later dismissed from the governorship by the Roman Emperor Tiberius because of his brutality) delays, gives the crowd an alternative choice, and then finally, with great reluctance, gives Jesus to the crowd to be crucified. Most New Testament scholars think that it is very difficult to get a precise historical picture of what happened at the crucifixion of Jesus—partly because the New Testament books reflect ongoing struggles between church and synagogue.

As nearly as can be determined from the information available it can be asserted that Jesus was crucified by Roman soldiers according to the decree of Pontius Pilate and that his death was called for by some of the citizens of Jerusalem. It is important to emphasize this one uncontestable historical fact—that Jesus was put to death by the authority of a Roman procurator and his execution was carried out according to Roman custom. Whether or not the Jewish Sanhedrin had the authority to sentence Jesus to death is a moot point. However, had he been put to death by the Jewish authorities he would undoubtedly have been stoned as was the Christian martyr Stephen, not crucified. In fact, under the Roman rule crucifixion had become a common form of execution in Palestine and the pattern was constant: the Jews were the crucified and the Romans the crucifiers. No one ever suggested, for example, that the Jews were responsible for the crucifixion of the two thieves who died on Calvary with Jesus.

To charge the Jews with deicide is grossly unfair for another reason. The charge is based upon the assumption that Jewish people in Jesus' time were guilty of his crucifixion. Common sense should refute this position. Most of the Jews in Jesus' time never heard of him. How can a Jew who lived in Rome or Alexandria or Corinth be considered guilty of the crucifixion of one of his kinsmen of whom he had never heard? The same may be said of Jews who lived in Palestine. How could a Jew in Galilee be held responsible for the death of Christ? It is even absurd to think that the Jews of Jerusalem were responsible for his death. And many who did come in contact with him had no idea of any messianic claims. Indeed Jesus appears to have asked his disciples not to tell anyone that he was the Messiah. In fact, the Gospels record that Jesus was kindly received in most places he visited. The Scriptures tell us that on Palm Sunday the Jews of Jerusalem welcomed Jesus into their city. Even if some of the Jews of Jerusalem turned against him within a few days, as Jesus painfully made his way to Calvary he was followed by a "great multitude of people," according to the author of Luke. He goes on to say that "the people stood by" and that after Jesus had breathed his last breath this great multitude returned to their homes "beating their breasts"—hardly a description of a people guilty of deicide.

But an even stronger case against the charge of deicide can be built upon the fact that while some Jews may have called for the crucifixion, others stood faithfully by him and psychologically and emotionally bore the cross with him. While Caiaphas was a Jew, so too was John, the beloved disciple, and Mary, the mother of Jesus, and Joseph of Arimathea, who provided the tomb. Had it not been for those Jews who accepted Jesus as the Messiah there would be no Christianity today. Obviously a blanket indictment of a whole people for the crucifixion of Jesus is unwarranted.

If it is granted that some of the people of Jerusalem called for and approved of the crucifixion of Jesus, why do we identify them by their Jewishness? Why not choose other characteristics? For example, could it not be said that all city people are responsible for the death of Jesus? Or that the religious establishment is guilty of deicide? Such accusations are no more absurd than the assumption that the Jews were guilty of the crime.

All such historical arguments overlook the theological objections to deicide. The first of such is the fact that Jesus while on the cross prayed, "Father, forgive them for they know not what they do." Surely there is something incongruous about Jesus' followers seeking someone on whom to place the blame, when Jesus himself sought to forgive. In addition, to assume that the guilt for one specific act can be passed from generation to generation and that the Jewish people of the twentieth century can be held responsible for the alleged acts of some first-century Jews is a denial of the Christian concept of individual responsibility.

The greatest distortion in the attempt to blame any particular group for the crucifixion is related to the belief of Christians that Christ died for all mankind. Those who participated in the crucifixion were not representative of either religion, race, occupation, or social position. They were, in fact, representative of all mankind. In that the cross of Jesus Christ is seen by Christians to have universal implications, any attempt to localize the responsibility for it is an attempt to evade its true meaning. No responsible theologian ever argued that Jesus died to forgive the sins of only those who were physically present or in some other way contributed to his crucifixion.

Hence it is important to recognize once and for all the fact that deicide has no foundation in Scripture or Christian theology. And furthermore it behooves Christian preachers and teachers to examine carefully their statements concerning the crucifixion of Jesus in order to guard against the inauthentic claim that the Jews are more guilty of the crucifixion than others.

Are the Jews Dispersed Because They Rejected Jesus?

One other common theological statement concerns the belief that the dispersion of the Jews was a result of their rejection of Jesus. This statement overlooks the fact that at the time of Jesus the Jews were already in a state of dispersion, that the majority of Jews in that day no longer lived in Palestine, as Palestine was already an occupied territory. The very reason for excitement at the coming of a Messiah was the Jewish hope that the Messiah would restore Palestine to them and establish a reign of peace upon the earth. To be sure the destruction of the Temple and the overthrow of Jerusalem by the Romans in A.D. 70–72 was a drastic blow to Judaism. Nevertheless the major dispersion described in the Christian Bible is not the dispersion of the Jews which was an historical process dating back as early as the fifth century before Christ, but the dispersion of Christianity from Jerusalem to the other centers of the Roman world.

From a purely pragmatic point of view, if anyone is going to argue seriously that the dispersion of the Jews from Palestine was the sign of God's wrath upon the Jews for their rejection of Jesus, how can it be explained that the Jews have in our age returned to Palestine—that Israel has been restored to them? And this restoration most assuredly has not followed their acceptance of Jesus as the Messiah. Then too, the Jews are not the only people who have rejected Jesus' claims to be the Messiah; why then have not all non-Christian groups faced dispersion? From the history of both the first century and the present day the dispersion of the Jews cannot be associated with their rejection of Jesus.

What Must Christians Do?

In the light of this, what is required is that Christians not only make public statements condemning anti-Semitism but that they mount an attack upon this form of group hatred in the local congregations. As history has shown all too clearly, Christian preaching and teaching have provided an atmosphere congenial to anti-Semitic feeling. Often the most derogatory remarks are made by persons who, with no intentional malice, have carelessly slandered Jews. I remember teaching a church school class in a small, poorly lighted room at the back of a country church. Seven or eight noisy, boisterous youngsters sat in front of me. There was a new boy in the class that morning, which was unusual. The lesson was on the crucifixion of Jesus. I told the boys how Jesus had gone to Jerusalem and there the Jews had taken him and had him crucified. We read the account of the Passion from the Gospel According to St. John, which verified my terminology: the Jews were the enemies of Jesus. I wasn't sure how well the boys had listened, and the moment the bell rang they all jumped to their feet and scurried out for the closing exercises—that is, everyone but the new boy. He stared down at the floor for a moment, then said to me in a whisper, "I thought you should know that I am a Jew."

I have often thought of that boy and wondered what must have been going on in his mind. Undoubtedly I had given him the impression that he was more guilty of the crucifixion of Jesus than anyone else in that classroom. What was he thinking of while I was glibly accusing the Jews of murder? What were the others boys thinking? Did they know that he was a Jew? Did they hold him—even in the vaguest way—responsible for what had happened to Jesus? My statements were made in ignorance. I was simply uninformed. Like so many Christians, I was cultivating the soil for the spread of the hatred of the Jews—hatred of the very people through whom, I, as a Christian, believed God had sent his Son.

If Christianity is to overcome the problem of its failure to relate authentically to the Jews it must begin by a massive assault on such common appalling accusations. The notion that the Jewish people of either Jesus' day or ours have a singular responsibility for the crucifixion must be avoided.

Finally, it is necessary not only to recognize the authenticity of the Covenant between God and Israel but to become aware of the fact that God has not rejected his people Israel. The American Catholic bishops urge Christians to recognize "the living and complex reality of Judaism after Jesus and the permanent election of Israel." With great expectation we should begin to discover what God has revealed to the world through the children of Abraham, Isaac, and Jacob—not only in the historical period between Abraham and Jesus, but also from the time of Jesus to the present day. St. Paul could not be more explicit in his affirmation that God has not rejected the Jews: "No! God has not rejected the people which he acknowledged of old as his own" (Romans 11:2).

This new day for Christian-Jewish relationships will be ushered in when we as Christians recognize the Jew, not as the villain of the Christian story, but as a Thou through whom God can speak to us.